The environment

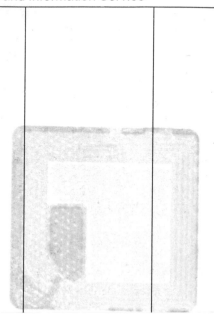

ROSIE HARLOW AND SALLY MORGAN

KING*f*ISHER

Contents

KINGFISHER
Kingfisher Publications Plc
New Penderel House
283-288 High Holborn
London WC1V 7HZ
www.kingfisherpub.com

Material in this edition
previously published by
Kingfisher Publications Plc
in the *Young Discoverers*
series
This edition published 2001

10 9 8 7 6 5 4 3 2 1

This concise edition
produced by PAGE*One*

Copyright © Kingfisher
Publications Plc 2001

1TR/0701/WKT/-(MAR)/128MA

A CIP catalogue record for
this book is available from
the British library.

ISBN 0 7534 0639 X

Printed in China

About This Book

This book looks at the damage we inflict on the world and suggests how we can help to make it a cleaner and safer place. It is filled with practical ideas and activities.

The first section, *Energy and Power*, explains how our environment is damaged by using too much energy.

Nature at Risk explains how our lifestyles destroy habitats and harm wildlife. It suggests ways that we can all help to protect plants and animals.

Pollution and Waste looks at the environmental damage caused by creating too much pollution.

Rubbish and Recycling tells you about the problems of producing too much rubbish and explains how recycling can help to improve the environment.

For all the experiments, you should be able to find most things around the home, garden or nearby woodland. You may have to buy some items, but they are all cheap and easy to find. After an experiment, return any wild creatures to where you found them. Sometimes you will need to ask an adult to help you. Wear rubber gloves whenever you handle rubbish or litter.

Remember: Be a Smart Scientist

- Before you begin an experiment, read the instructions carefully and collect all the things you need.

- Put on some old clothes or wear an overall.

- When you have finished, clear everything away, especially sharp things like knives and scissors, and wash your hands.

- Keep a record of what you do and what you find out.

- If your results are not quite the same as those in this book, do not worry. See if you can work out what has happened, and why.

ENERGY AND POWER

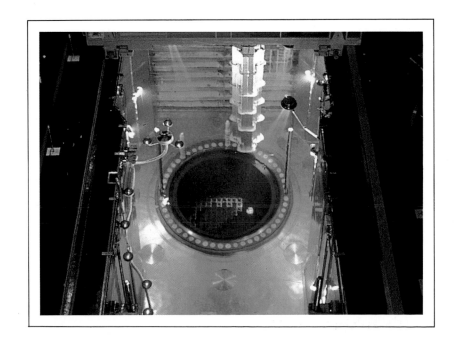

What is Energy?

Energy is everywhere. We can see it as light, hear it as sound and feel it as heat. There are other forms of energy as well, such as electrical, chemical and movement energy. We use electrical energy for power in our homes, and chemical energy, in the form of fuel, to power our cars. But, as you will see, when we use energy, we often do harm to our environment as well.

Lightning is a giant spark of electricity. The energy from a single flash would be enough to light a town for one year.

factory

bicycles

tanker

house

We use electrical energy to heat and light factories, offices, schools and homes. Electricity is also used to light up our streets at night.

Do it yourself

See how energy can be used to make things turn. You must ask an adult to help you when you light the candle.

1. Draw a snake like the one shown here on a piece of paper. Cut it out and add a red tongue and two eyes. Then tie a length of thread on to the snake's head.

2. Hang your snake above a lighted candle, keeping its tail well away from the flame. Now watch it turn. (Be sure to blow out the candle when you have finished.)

How It Works

When a candle burns, two forms of energy are created – heat and light. The heat causes the air to rise up which in turn makes the snake spin round.

pen

red tongue

scissors

coloured paper

candle

The energy needed to turn the pedals of a bicycle comes from the cyclist. Cars and lorries get their energy from fuels such as petrol and diesel, and some homes are heated using fuel oil. These fuels are delivered in special vehicles called tankers.

office block

lorry

street lighting

cars

petrol station

Food for Energy

People use energy to move, keep warm, grow and stay healthy. The energy we need comes from the food we eat.

7

Generating Power

Energy can be changed from one form into another. For example, when electricity passes through a light bulb, electrical energy is changed into heat and light energy. Most of the electricity we use today is made in power stations. But power stations need a source of energy too. This usually comes from fuels such as oil, gas and coal. Inside the power station, the chemical energy in the fuel is changed into electrical energy.

Eye-Spy

Use the energy in your muscles to light up a bulb by fitting a dynamo light set to your bicycle. When you ride your bicycle, the wheels turn and a tiny generator inside the dynamo makes electricity.

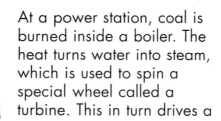

cooling tower cools steam

boiler

steam

cables carry electricity

pylon

coal supply

steam spins turbine

generator makes electricity

At a power station, coal is burned inside a boiler. The heat turns water into steam, which is used to spin a special wheel called a turbine. This in turn drives a machine called a generator, which changes the movement energy into electrical energy. Power cables, supported by pylons, carry the electricity to homes and factories.

Do it yourself

Make your own steam turbine. You'll need an adult to help you.

1. Cut a circle 8cm across from a thick foil food tray. Pierce a small hole in the centre, then snip in towards the hole with your scissors as shown. Twist the sections slightly to make the blades.

2. Ask an adult to punch two small holes in the top of a full, soft drinks can – one in the centre, the other about 15mm to one side. Empty the drink out and pour about 100ml of water into the can.

Many power stations have cooling towers. The hot steam cools inside the towers and turns back into water. The water is then pumped back to the boiler where it is heated all over again.

3. To make the stand, cut a piece of thick foil 20cm long and 4cm wide. Fold it in half lengthways, then bend it into shape as shown so that it fits across the top of the can. Make a small hole 5cm up on each side of the stand.

4. Fix the stand on to the can with a small screw. Then push a 10cm long cocktail or barbecue stick through the holes in the sides of the stand, threading the wheel in place as you go.

5. Make sure the blades of the wheel are positioned over the small hole in the can. Then ask an adult to put your turbine on a gas cooker over a low heat. As the water starts to boil, the escaping steam will spin the wheel on your turbine.

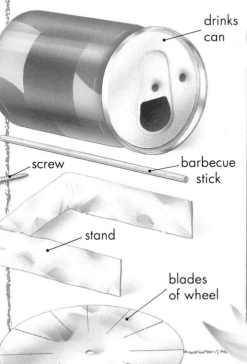

drinks can

screw

barbecue stick

stand

blades of wheel

heat

9

The Price of Power

When fuels are burned to give energy, they release harmful gases that pollute (poison) our air. Often these gases lie above cities, creating a layer of smog (dirty air). Some of the gases mix with water in the air to form acids. When it rains, the acid in the rain damages forests and lakes. Burning fuel also releases the gas carbon dioxide. This is called a 'greenhouse gas' because it traps the Sun's heat in the atmosphere (the air around the Earth), just like glass traps heat in a greenhouse. The trapped heat makes the atmosphere warm up, which may cause changes in our weather.

Many children suffer from an illness called asthma. They find it hard to breathe and have to use an inhaler. Doctors think that air pollution may be causing the asthma.

Then and Now

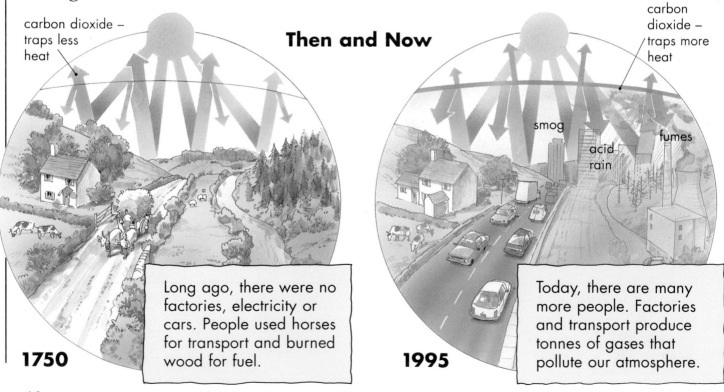

carbon dioxide – traps less heat

carbon dioxide – traps more heat

smog

acid rain

fumes

1750 Long ago, there were no factories, electricity or cars. People used horses for transport and burned wood for fuel.

1995 Today, there are many more people. Factories and transport produce tonnes of gases that pollute our atmosphere.

Do it yourself

Try making a smog in a glass jar. You'll need to ask an adult to light the paper for you.

1. Find a large jar and wash it out with water. Don't dry the jar though – you want it to be slightly damp.

damp jar

ice

foil

twist of paper

A thick layer of smog hangs over New York City, USA, making it difficult to see the buildings clearly.

How It Works

The smoke from the burning paper rises up in the warm air. When it reaches the cold air around the ice, it sinks back down to the middle where it mixes with the water in the air to form a smog. When the weather is damp and warm, the same happens over cities that produce a lot of smoke and pollution.

smog

2. Cut a piece of kitchen foil slightly larger than the top of your jar. Put some ice cubes on to the foil.

3. Cut a small piece of newspaper. Fold it a couple of times then twist it up.

4. Ask an adult to light the paper and drop it in the jar. Quickly seal the jar with the foil and ice and watch what happens. (Don't worry if the flame goes out.)

The Car Crisis

The car is our most popular form of transport. Every day, across the world, more than 100,000 new cars appear on the roads. But every time we use a car we add more pollution to the atmosphere. This pollution is particularly bad in cities where rush hour traffic fills the streets. It is caused by the cars' exhaust fumes which are made up of harmful gases such as sulphur dioxide, carbon monoxide and nitrogen oxides. They also contain tiny bits of soot. To cut down on air pollution we must design cars that are cleaner to run, and use our cars less often.

Rush hour traffic in Bangkok, Thailand, produces so much pollution that a dirty layer of smog hangs over the city.

How Can We Help?

- Walk or use a bicycle on short journeys.
- Use public transport instead of a car as much as possible.
- On regular journeys, see if your family can pair up with another family and use one car instead of two.

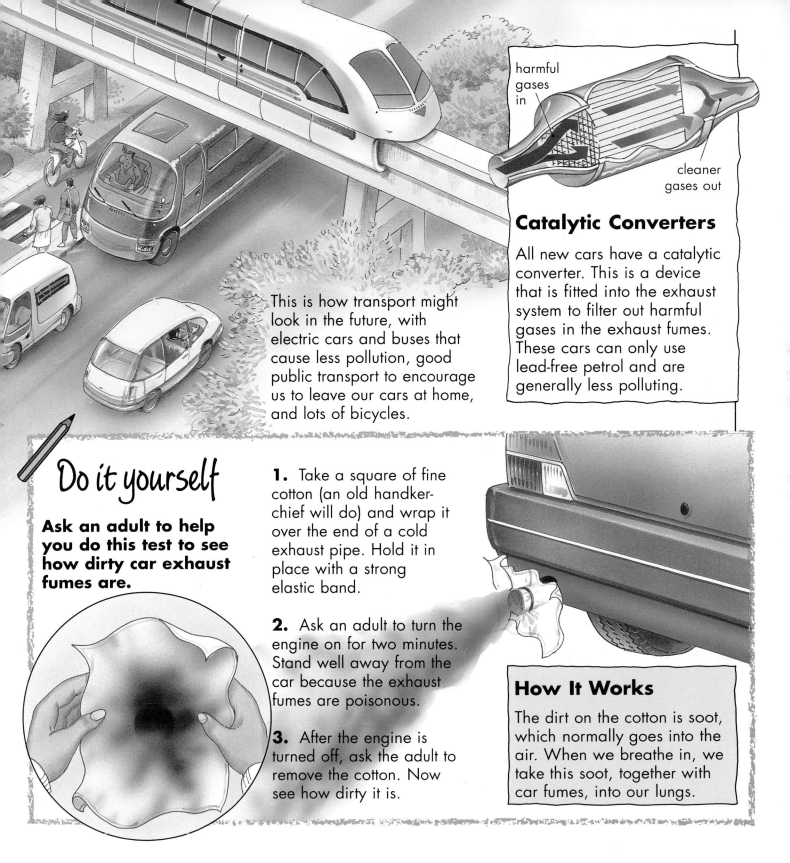

This is how transport might look in the future, with electric cars and buses that cause less pollution, good public transport to encourage us to leave our cars at home, and lots of bicycles.

Catalytic Converters

harmful gases in

cleaner gases out

All new cars have a catalytic converter. This is a device that is fitted into the exhaust system to filter out harmful gases in the exhaust fumes. These cars can only use lead-free petrol and are generally less polluting.

Do it yourself

Ask an adult to help you do this test to see how dirty car exhaust fumes are.

1. Take a square of fine cotton (an old handkerchief will do) and wrap it over the end of a cold exhaust pipe. Hold it in place with a strong elastic band.

2. Ask an adult to turn the engine on for two minutes. Stand well away from the car because the exhaust fumes are poisonous.

3. After the engine is turned off, ask the adult to remove the cotton. Now see how dirty it is.

How It Works

The dirt on the cotton is soot, which normally goes into the air. When we breathe in, we take this soot, together with car fumes, into our lungs.

13

Nature's Fuels

All living things depend on the Sun for energy. Plants use light energy to make their own food – a form of chemical energy. Animals eat plants so they can use the chemical energy stored inside. The fuels we all depend on – coal, gas and oil – also contain a store of chemical energy. They are called 'fossil' fuels because their energy comes from organisms (plants and animals) that lived millions of years ago. When the organisms died their bodies became buried and their remains slowly turned into coal, gas and oil.

Oil Underground

Oil is the fossil remains of tiny animals that died millions of years ago. Oil rigs drill down below the ground or sea bed and remove the oil.

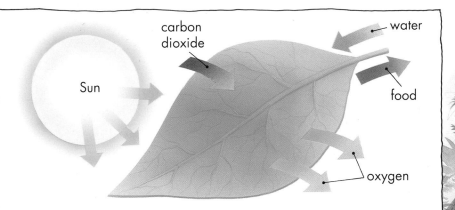

carbon dioxide

water

Sun

food

oxygen

Energy from the Sun

Plants capture light energy from the Sun and use it to make food in a process called photosynthesis. Inside the leaves, the gas carbon dioxide is combined with water to make sugars and a substance called starch. The gas oxygen is produced and released back into the air.

Do it yourself

Do this simple experiment to see whether or not plants need light to grow.

1. Put some damp cotton wool on three glass jar lids and sprinkle a few cress seeds on top.

2. Put one lid on a sunny windowsill, another in a dark cupboard. Cut a small hole in a cardboard box and put the third lid inside. Close up the box.

3. Leave the seeds to grow for a week, keeping the cotton wool damp with a little water.

How It Works

The seeds on the windowsill grow well because they have enough light. Those in the cupboard shrivel and die because, without light, they cannot make food and grow. The seeds in the box grow towards the hole to get as much light as possible.

Coal is the remains of plants that lived in swamps millions of years ago. As the plants died, they sunk layer upon layer beneath the water. The weight of the top layers squashed the bottom layer which eventually became much harder, forming coal.

coal seam

👁 Eye-Spy

Next time you eat bread, cereal, potatoes, pasta or rice, think about where the food has come from. All these foods contain starch made by plants from the Sun's energy.

15

Other Natural Fuels

Coal, oil and gas are not the only fuels that nature gives us. In some parts of the world, such as Ireland and Siberia, people still use a substance called peat. Peat is the first stage in the long coal-making process. It is softer than coal and not as rich in energy, but it can be burned for fuel, and is sometimes used in power stations to generate electricity. Wood also makes a good fuel – many people still use it to heat their homes and for cooking.

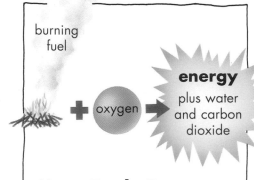

burning fuel + oxygen → **energy** plus water and carbon dioxide

How Fuels Burn

As we have seen, fuels contain a store of chemical energy. When fuels burn they react with oxygen in the air and release heat and light energy, plus water and carbon dioxide. The proper word to describe something burning in air is combustion.

Digging for Fuel

Peat is still an important fuel in Ireland, where it is dug up from the ground as small brick-like pieces. The peat bricks are then dried before being burned on fires and stoves in the home.

Wood is an important fuel in poor countries where it is collected and burned on fires and stoves for cooking food and boiling water.

Low on Fuels

Unfortunately, there is only a limited amount of fossil fuels in the world. Once the supplies have run out they cannot be replaced. This is why fossil fuels are called non-renewable fuels. Wood is also being used up too quickly. Trees can be replanted but they still take over 50 years to grow. So we need to find alternative sources of energy if we are not to run out of power.

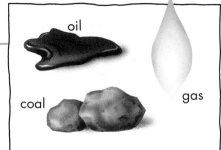

oil

gas

coal

How Much Is Left?

There may be enough coal to last for another 300 years. But oil and gas may run out within the next 50 years.

Do it yourself

Make some paper logs to burn as fuel.

1. Tear some newspaper into strips and put them in a large bowl of hot water. Mash the paper into a pulp with a wooden spoon.

2. Scoop up the pulp using a sieve. Pick up a handful of pulp and squeeze out all the water, forming a log shape as you do so.

3. Make several more logs, then leave them to dry out. Then ask an adult to help you make a fire with them.

How Can We Help?

If we all use less energy then the supply of fossil fuels will last longer. Try to turn off unwanted lights, use the car less often, and wear an extra sweater instead of turning the heating up.

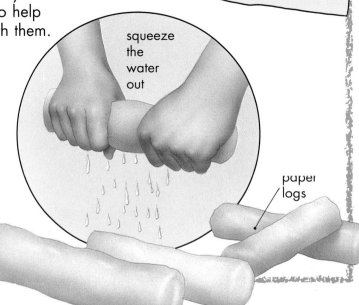

newspaper strips

squeeze the water out

paper logs

Splitting Atoms

Instead of using fossil fuels to make electricity, we can use 'nuclear power'. The energy for nuclear power comes from a metal called uranium. Like all matter, uranium is made up of tiny particles called atoms. When a uranium atom is split into smaller particles a vast amount of heat energy is released. This can be used to generate electricity. But waste products from nuclearpower stations are very dangerous and are difficult to get rid of safely.

Radioactive Waste

Nuclear power produces a dangerous form of energy called radioactivity. This can contaminate (infect) people and animals, making them very sick. Radioactive waste from power stations is marked with this warning symbol.

Energy from Atoms

neutron fired at atom

atom splits

heat energy produced

neutrons released

Sun's surface

In a nuclear reaction, tiny particles called neutrons are fired at uranium atoms at very high speeds. They split the uranium atoms, causing them to release more neutrons and lots of heat energy. The neutrons bump into more uranium atoms, causing them to split. This is called a fission reaction. Another type of nuclear reaction, called nuclear fusion, is taking place on the Sun's surface all the time.

If there has been a leak at a nuclear power station, scientists use a machine called a Geiger counter to test for radioactivity in the ground and in animals. Sometimes farmers paint their sheep yellow to show they have been contaminated with radioactivity.

The reactor core in a nuclear power station is surrounded by water. The water is heated by the nuclear reaction.

Making Electricity

In a nuclear power station, the uranium is placed in rods inside a 'reactor core'. It is carefully shielded so that the radioactivity cannot escape. The heat from the nuclear reaction heats the water surrounding the core. This hot water is then used to turn water in the heat exchanger into steam. The steam is used to spin the turbines, and electricity is generated.

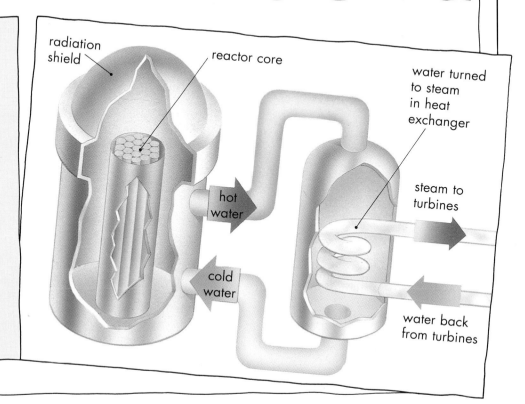

radiation shield

reactor core

water turned to steam in heat exchanger

hot water

steam to turbines

cold water

water back from turbines

Energy from the Sun

The Sun is like a huge power station releasing vast amounts of heat and light energy. It supplies a free source of energy that will not run out. Scientists have devised many new ways of making use of solar energy. Solar panels absorb heat from the Sun, and heat water for homes and factories. Other panels, called photovoltaics, can change light directly into electricity. Both of these ways of using solar energy produce very little pollution.

👁 Eye-Spy

On a hot sunny day, a garden hose pipe acts like a solar panel. It absorbs the Sun's energy and the water inside heats up. Look out for a cat lying on a hose pipe, enjoying the heat.

Do it yourself

Make some tea using energy from the Sun.

1. Take two clear glass bottles the same size. Paint one of them black. Put two tea bags in each bottle and fill them up with cold water.

2. Put the bottles on a sunny windowsill for at least six hours. If you have a thermometer, test the temperature of the water every two hours to see which bottle heats up quickest. Watch the water turn brown as your tea brews.

tea bags

water

thermometer

How It Works

The Sun's energy heats the water and brews the tea. Because the black glass absorbs heat better than the clear glass, the water in the black bottle will heat up faster and the tea will brew more quickly.

Trapping the Sun's Energy

Simple solar panels like the one in the diagram are placed on the roof of a house and used to heat water. The water absorbs heat as it circulates through the pipes in the panel, and becomes much hotter.

On a much larger scale, this solar power station in California does the same thing. Thousands of mirrors reflect the sunlight on to tubes containing a special oil. The oil is heated to 575°C and is used to make steam which, in turn, spins a turbine to make electricity.

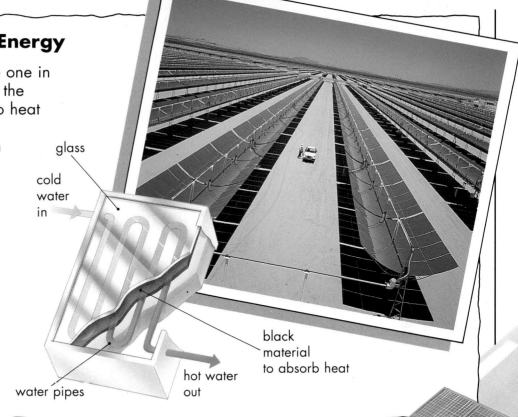

glass

cold water in

water pipes

hot water out

black material to absorb heat

Called the Sunraycer, this strange-looking car is powered by solar energy. It won the first international solar-powered car race in 1987, travelling more than 3,140km across Australia.

👁 Eye-Spy

Look out for small items powered by solar energy, such as calculators, watches and radios. They use photovoltaic cells to convert the light energy into electricity.

Wind Power

The wind is another free source of energy that can be trapped and used to make electricity. People have made use of wind power for hundreds of years. Windmills were once built to turn a large millstone that was used to grind wheat into flour. Small wind-powered pumps are still used to pump water from wells. About 25 years ago, the first modern wind generators appeared in the USA. Since then, many more have been built all around the world. Because the wind will never stop blowing, wind power is an important source of renewable energy.

Windmills

Traditional windmills for grinding wheat are still found in countries such as Holland. This windmill has four large sails to catch the wind.

Wind Farms

A collection of wind generators is called a wind farm. This one is in California, USA, on the mountains behind the city of Los Angeles. It is very windy here, so the area is ideal for wind power.

On a wind farm, each generator has two or three long narrow blades. As the blades turn in the wind, they turn a turbine which generates electricity.

Do it yourself

Make this wind-powered winch and see how you can use the power of the wind to lift objects into the air.

1. Tape a cotton reel on its side to the top of a length of wood about 25cm long.

2. Cut four pieces of card measuring 5cm x 3cm for your blades. Tape each blade on to the end of a cocktail stick as shown. Then stick the other end of the cocktail sticks into a cork and twist the blades so that they face each other.

3. Stick the cork on to the sharp end of a pencil. Thread the pencil through the cotton reel on the wooden stand. Make sure the pencil turns freely in the hole.

4. Jam a slightly smaller cotton reel (complete with thread) on to the blunt end of the pencil. If the hole is too big, bind the end of the pencil with paper to give a tight fit.

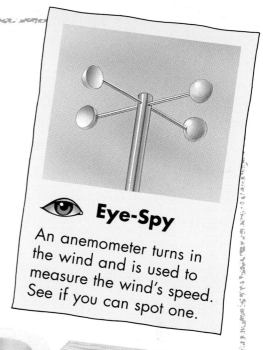

Eye-Spy

An anemometer turns in the wind and is used to measure the wind's speed. See if you can spot one.

materials

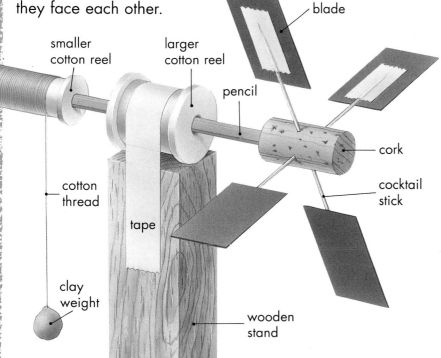

smaller cotton reel

larger cotton reel

pencil

blade

cork

cotton thread

cocktail stick

tape

clay weight

wooden stand

5. Unravel about 20cm of thread from the smaller cotton reeel and tie a blob of modelling clay on the end to act as a weight.

6. Blow on the blades to see if your winch can lift the weight. You may need to alter the direction of the blades, or make the weight slightly smaller, to get your machine to work properly. Now try your machine outside in the wind.

The Power of Water

Moving water is an important source of free energy. Hundreds of years ago people built watermills by rivers and used them to grind wheat into flour, just like a windmill. Today, moving water can be used to generate electricity. Huge dams, called hydroelectric dams, are built across rivers to generate electricity for nearby cities. The waters of the ocean are also moving, and waves and tides are now being used as a source of energy.

Hydroelectric dams are built across rivers where there is a steep fall in height. The water falling from the top of the dam turns a huge turbine to make electricity.

Do it yourself

Try making your own waterwheel out of a plastic drinks bottle. You may need to ask an adult to help you if you find some of the cutting too difficult.

1. Cut a plastic drinks bottle into three pieces as shown. The middle section should be 8cm deep. Now cut four strips, 2cm wide, out of the middle piece. Cut each strip in half to give eight blades.

plastic drinks bottle

blades

cork

middle section

base section

2. Draw eight lines evenly spaced down the side of a cork. Cut slits down the lines with a blunt knife and push a blade into each slit.

This is a tidal barrage, designed to trap the power of the tides. It is built across the mouth of a river, near the sea. As the tide moves up or down the river, the water passes over a turbine, causing it to turn and generate electricity.

turbine

Wave generators (above) are built on the coast. The waves are funnelled up a special ramp, forcing air through the turbines to make electricity.

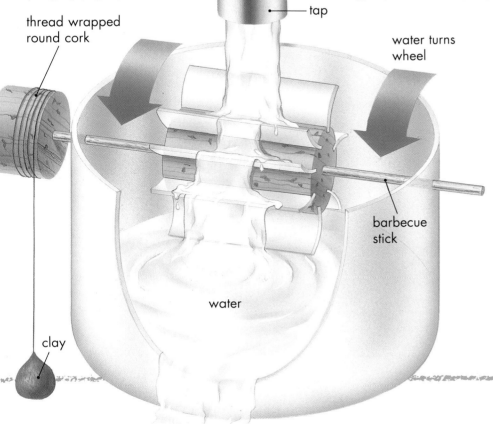

thread wrapped round cork

tap

water turns wheel

barbecue stick

water

clay

3. Cut away a section of the bottle base as shown. Then pierce two holes just below the rim, one on either side.

4. Cut a wooden barbecue stick in half. Feed each half through a hole and push the sticks into the ends of the cork.

5. Put a second cork on the end of one of the sticks. Tie a length of thread round it and attach a blob of modelling clay. Now put your water-wheel under a tap. Slowly turn the tap on and watch your machine lift the weight.

Energy in the Home

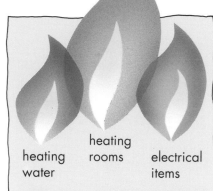

Every home uses energy, but what is it needed for? Modern homes are wired so that electricity can be carried to each room, providing power for lights and items such as televisions and kettles. Fuels such as oil, gas and coal may also be burned in boilers to provide hot water for central heating and for washing. Some equipment is battery-powered. Batteries are stores of energy which contain chemicals that react together to form an electric current. Some batteries can be recharged many times using a power source such as the Sun or electricity.

heating water   heating rooms   electrical items

Where Does It Go?

More than half the energy we use at home goes on heating rooms. A quarter is used to power electrical items and a fifth is used to heat water for washing.

The modern bedroom is very energy-hungry! We use batteries to power toys, and run televisions and radios on electricity.

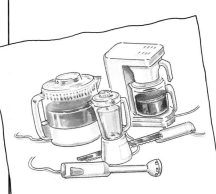

Eye-Spy

Kitchens use up a lot of energy. Can you work out why? To help you, count the number of electrical items in your kitchen. How many are there compared with your bedroom?

NATURE AT RISK

Where Animals Live

Plants and animals are found almost everywhere on Earth – in the air, on the land, underground and in the water. Each living thing belongs to a particular kind of place, called its habitat. For example, cacti grow in the desert, jellyfish are found in the sea, parrots live in tropical forests. When people cut down trees to make way for roads and farms, or pour harmful chemicals into the environment, they damage these habitats and destroy the wildlife.

There are many different types of habitat in the world, from the tropical rainforests to the polar ice caps. This picture shows the kind of animals that live in some of these habitats.

Reefs at Risk

Coral reefs are home to many sea creatures and plants. Unfortunately, they are threatened by people who are polluting the oceans and damaging their habitat.

tropical rainforest
jaguar

grassland
gazelle

deciduous woodland
woodmouse

river
trout

Do it yourself

Find out what type of habitat woodlice like best.

1. First, find some woodlice by looking under logs and bark.

2. Then spread a thin layer of cotton wool on to a small tray or box lid. Number the four quarters of the tray with labels as shown here.

3. Cover half the tray with newspaper while you spray areas 1 and 2 with water. The cotton wool should be damp but not soaking wet.

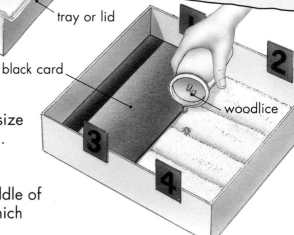

water spray

cotton wool

newspaper

tray or lid

black card

woodlice

4. Lay a piece of black paper cut to size over areas 1 and 3.

5. Now put your woodlice in the middle of the tray and see which area they go to.

How It Works

You have divided the tray into four areas – (1) dark and damp, (2) light and damp, (3) dark and dry, and (4) light and dry. Woodlice prefer dark, damp habitats, so they will go to area 1.

mountain
eagle

polar regions
polar bear

ocean
whale

coniferous forest
wolf

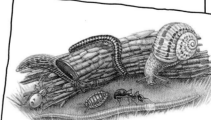

👁 Eye-Spy

If you want to see some animals in their natural habitat, turn over a log in your garden or local park. How many different creatures can you find?

Keeping the Balance

Plants and animals that share the same habitat rely on each other for their survival. A delicate balance exists between them that depends largely on the amount of food available. Plants are able to make their own food, but animals have to find ready-made food. Some animals only eat plants – they are called herbivores. Other animals feed off the plant-eaters. These are the carnivores, or meat-eaters. But the balance is easily upset. For example, if fishermen catch too many sand eels, the seabirds that feed on the eels may die because they have no more food.

People upset the balance of nature when they cut down large areas of forest. The animals whose lives depend on the trees for food and shelter soon die.

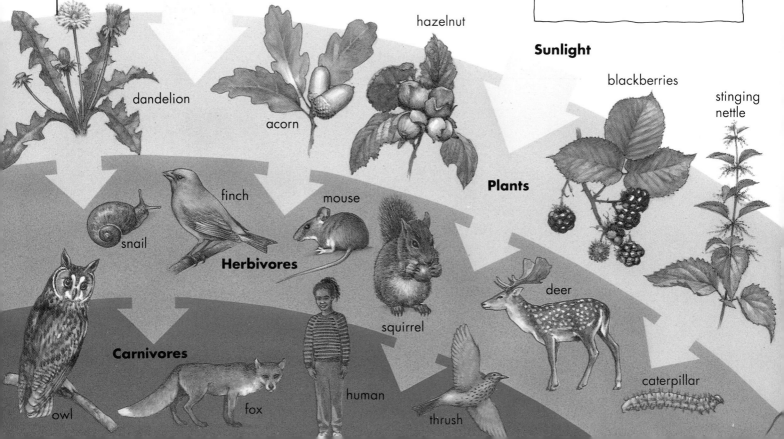

hazelnut

Sunlight

dandelion

acorn

blackberries

stinging nettle

Plants

finch

mouse

snail

Herbivores

squirrel

deer

Carnivores

owl

fox

human

thrush

caterpillar

Do it yourself

See a food chain in action.

1. Find a small leafy shoot that has a few greenfly on it. (Try looking on roses or nasturtiums.) Put the shoot into a small bottle of water and plug the mouth of the bottle with tissue paper.

2. Put the bottle in a large glass jar. Cover the top with thin woven fabric – from an old handkerchief or a pair of tights. Use an elastic band to hold it in place.

3. Watch the greenfly for a few days through a magnifying glass. Can you see them sucking juices out of the plant?

4. Now put a ladybird into the jar and watch it feed off the greenfly. Which animal is the herbivore and which is the carnivore?

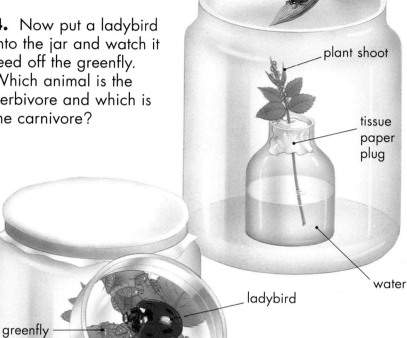

plant shoot

tissue paper plug

water

ladybird

greenfly

grass

A Woodland Food Web

This diagram on the left shows 'what eats what' in a woodland habitat. Energy for life begins with the Sun. Plants use the energy from sunlight to make food. Herbivores (in the orange band) eat the plants and are then eaten by the carnivores. Try to pick out a simple food chain, for example, an acorn is eaten by a mouse which is then eaten by an owl. Can you work out any other food chains? (Turn to page 32 for some more examples.)

A Delicate Balance

Kestrels are predators of mice – that is, they feed on them. When there are lots of mice the kestrel has plenty of food and produces many young. But if the mouse population goes down, so does the number of kestrels.

31

Pollution Problems

One of the many threats to our wildlife is waste. In nature, waste materials such as dead plants and animals are quickly broken down and recycled. But much of the waste we produce is harmful and difficult to get rid of. Harmful waste is called pollution. Some of the most damaging pollution is caused by factories and cars. They produce fumes that turn the rain into acid. Acid rain has killed millions of trees. If we want to protect our environment we must learn to cut down on the amount of pollution we are producing.

You can see waste almost everywhere you look – in the home, on the roads, in cities and on farms. Rubbish is buried in the countryside, liquid waste is poured into rivers and oceans, and harmful fumes are pumped into the air.

acid rain

factory fumes

farming chemicals

rubbish

transport fumes

liquid waste from factories

Litter That Kills

Litter can be dangerous to wildlife. Sometimes small animals, such as mice and voles, climb into bottles, only to find they cannot get out again. Without food, they soon starve to death.

How Can We Help?

- Don't drop litter. It may be a death-trap.
- Cut down on pollution by using the car less. Ride a bicycle or walk on short journeys.
- If you spot bad pollution, write a letter of complaint to your council.

Algal Blooms

Sometimes you may find a thick green blanket of algae (tiny plants) floating on a river or pond. This is called an algal bloom. Eventually it leads to the death of fish living in the water. An algal bloom occurs when fertilizers from local farmland drain into a river or pond, causing the algae to grow very fast.

Do it yourself

Find out how polluted your local stream or pond is by discovering which creatures live in the water.

Sweep a dipping net through the water to catch some tiny animals. Use this chart to identify your animals and find out how polluted the water is.

Some animals can only live in unpolluted water. If you find these, you know your water is clean. Others can survive in badly polluted water.

WHAT TO LOOK FOR		
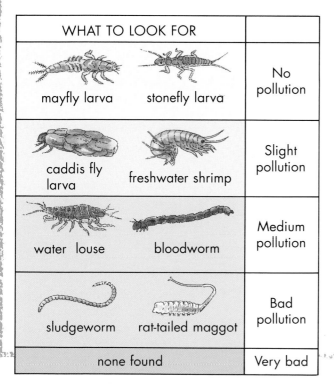 mayfly larva	stonefly larva	No pollution
caddis fly larva	freshwater shrimp	Slight pollution
water louse	bloodworm	Medium pollution
sludgeworm	rat-tailed maggot	Bad pollution
none found		Very bad

Turn to page 15 to find out how to make and use a dipping net.

Forests in Danger

Trees are very useful plants. As well as being home to a wealth of wildlife, their wood can be used for making paper, for building homes and furniture, and as fuel. Also, when plants make food from sunlight, they use up a gas called carbon dioxide and release the gas oxygen. People breathe in oxygen and breathe out carbon dioxide, and trees help to balance the level of these gases in the air. Yet all around the world forests are rapidly being destroyed for timber or to grow crops.

More than half the world's rainforests have already been destroyed. If we continue to cut them down, there will be no forests left 50 years from now.

👁 Eye-Spy

Go into each room at home and see how many things you can find that come from trees. Here are some ideas.

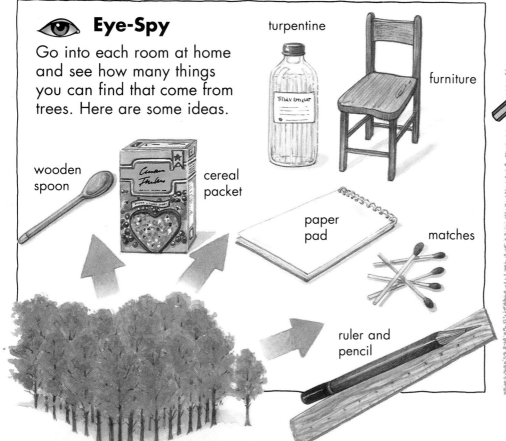

turpentine

furniture

wooden spoon

cereal packet

paper pad

matches

ruler and pencil

Do it yourself

Show that plants give off a gas.

1. Fill a bowl or glass tank with water. Put a glass or jar into the water and tip it up so that all the air escapes.

2. Place some pondweed in the glass without letting any air back in. (You can buy pondweed from a pet shop.)

Drugs from the Forest

Did you know that many of our medicines are made from plants that grow in the rainforest? Drugs made from this rosy periwinkle are used to treat leukemia. Unless we save the remaining rainforests, we will lose many useful plants that could save lives.

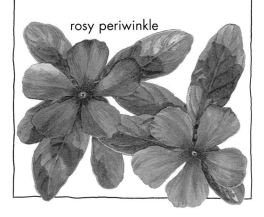
rosy periwinkle

Rainforests are home to at least three-quarters of all the world's wildlife. Millions of different kinds of plants and animals live there, but many of them have not yet been discovered.

How Can We Help?

- Don't waste paper – you are also wasting trees.
- Collect newspapers and cardboard for recycling.
- When people buy new furniture, they should check that it is not made of wood from the rainforests, such as teak and mahogany.

4. Leave the tank for a few days in a warm sunny place. Watch the gas bubbling off the plant and collecting at the top of the glass. This gas is oxygen, produced by the plant as it makes food.

3. Turn the glass upside down in the water and sit it on three small blobs of modelling clay. Make sure you leave a small gap underneath the glass.

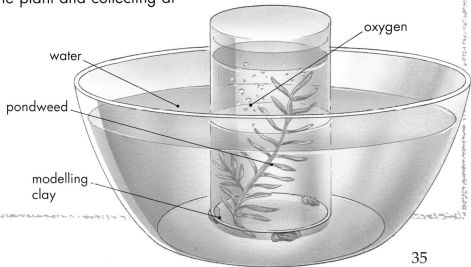

water

oxygen

pondweed

modelling clay

Rivers, Ponds and Lakes

Clean fresh water is home to a wide variety of wildlife. Animals such as fish, snails, crayfish and insects live in the water itself, dragonflies and mayflies skim across the surface, water birds live close by, and water plants flourish on the banks. But many of our rivers, ponds and lakes have become polluted by waste chemicals that pour into them from farms and factories. Sometimes only the hardiest plants and animals survive in the filthy water.

A healthy river is teeming with wildlife living in and around the water. A polluted stretch of river has little life in it. The dirty water often smells and may be full of all kinds of litter. An algal bloom may float on the water's surface.

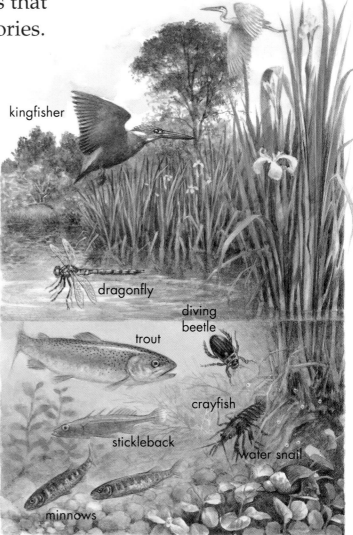

heron

iris

kingfisher

dragonfly

diving beetle

trout

crayfish

stickleback

water snail

minnows

Fisherman's Threat

Waterbirds sometimes get tangled in fishing lines left on riverbanks by careless fishermen. The birds may die if the line gets too tight around their throats.

algal bloom

litter

Clean-Up Campaign

Many young people spend some of their spare time helping to clean up their local river or pond, making it much safer for wildlife. Find out if there is a clean-up campaign near you that you can join.

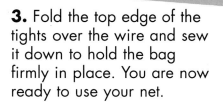

Do it yourself

Make your own pond dipping net.

1. Ask an adult to cut a piece off a metal coat hanger about 70cm long. Bend the wire into a circle leaving 5cm at each end, then poke the ends into a bamboo stick. Tape the ring in place with insulating tape.

2. Cut the legs off a pair of tights. Sew the cut edges together to make a 'bag' out of the waist part.

3. Fold the top edge of the tights over the wire and sew it down to hold the bag firmly in place. You are now ready to use your net.

4. Take a large plastic container with you to keep your animals in, plus a magnifying glass. When you have caught some animals in your net, do not pick them up with your fingers – you may squash them. Instead, turn the net inside out and lower it into the water inside the container. Always put the animals back when you have finished looking at them.

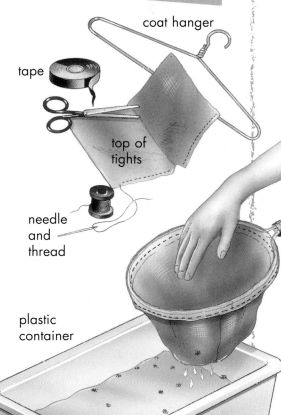

coat hanger

tape

top of tights

needle and thread

plastic container

dipping net

magnifying glass

Save Our Seas

Today, our seas are under threat. We rely on the seas to provide us with food, particularly fish. But we are catching far too many fish, so their numbers are going down rapidly. Pollution, too, is a problem. For many years, people thought that getting rid of waste at sea was safe and that it would be quickly diluted. But poisons build up in the water and affect the health of sea animals. All over the world, dolphins and seals are dying from new diseases and fish are found with strange-looking growths on their skin.

Pacific Ocean

Almost three-quarters of the Earth's surface is covered by water. Yet we manage to pollute much of it and take fish stocks dangerously low.

Animals such as dolphins, turtles and sharks often get caught up in fishing nets. Purse seine nets are like huge bags, whereas drift nets are more like curtains. Both of these nets can be death-traps. Long lines are much better because they only catch the fish that are wanted.

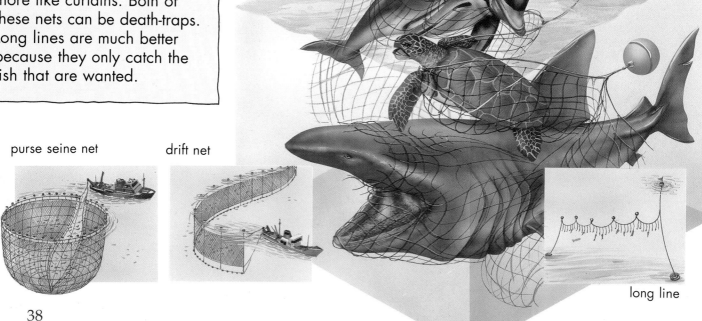

purse seine net

drift net

long line

Do it yourself

Do this simple test to see how oil damages a bird's feathers.

1. Collect two feathers. Then rub a few drops of bicycle oil or lubricating oil on to one of the feathers using some cotton wool.

2. Pour a few drops of water on to each feather and see what happens.

clean feather

oily feather

feather

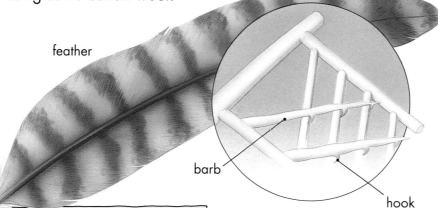

barb

hook

How It Works

The drops of water on the clean feather roll off because the feather is waterproof. The oil destroys the waterproofing, so the water soaks into the oily feather and spoils its shape. Birds with oily feathers cannot fly or dive and soon die from cold and hunger.

More Things To Try

The barbs of a feather are attached to one another with hooks, rather like Velcro. Oil damages the feathers so that the hooks no longer work and the bird cannot fly.

You can see the hooks on a feather by using a magnifying glass. Try breaking the hooks apart and then joining them up again like a zip. This zip effect is useful, because even if the feathers break apart in stormy weather, the bird can always 'zip' them up again by preening them into shape.

Oil tankers move millions of tonnes of oil around the world each year. When there is an accident, oil spills into the sea where it causes terrible damage to wildlife. Thousands of seabirds may die. If the birds are rescued quickly, the oil can be removed from their feathers by washing them carefully in detergents such as washing-up liquid.

Farming Takes Over

The number of people in the world has increased rapidly over the last two hundred years, and it is still increasing. All these extra mouths need food to eat, and farming has had to keep up with the demand. Natural habitats are destroyed to make way for huge fields. Chemicals are sprayed on to the fields to increase the yield (output). There are fertilizers to feed the crops, and pesticides to kill pests. But these chemicals cause pollution, and pesticides kill more than just the pests.

Free-Range

Many farm animals live indoors, packed together with no room to move. But some farmers let their animals roam free outdoors. These animals are called free-range.

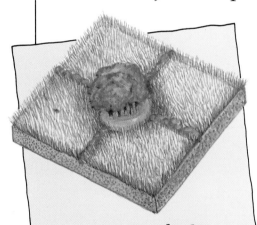

Natural Pockets

To avoid using harmful pesticides, some farmers grow small pockets of woodland in the corners of their fields. Many of the animals that live there feed on the pests.

On a farm, the huge fields are usually planted with a single crop and sprayed with chemicals. Few plants and animals are found living here.

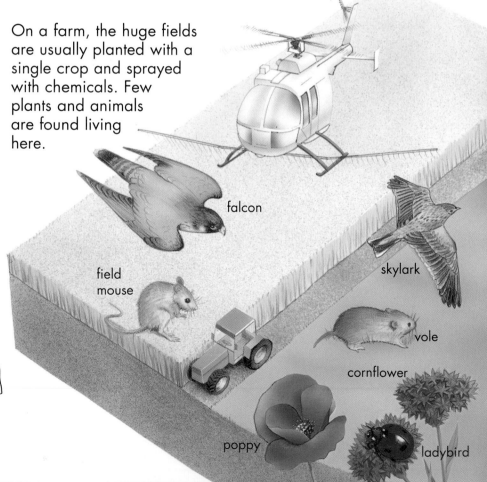

falcon

field mouse

skylark

vole

cornflower

poppy

ladybird

Combine harvesters are used to cut down crops. But they also destroy small animals that get in their way.

In comparison to farmland, natural meadows and woodlands are rich in wildlife. It is important to protect these habitats.

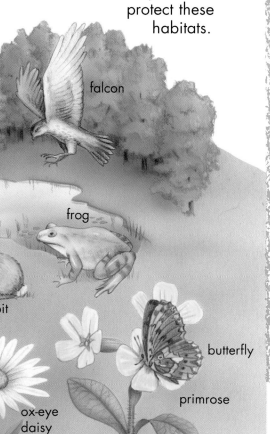

falcon

frog

obit

butterfly

primrose

ox-eye daisy

Do it yourself

Worms are farmers' friends. As they burrow through the soil, they mix it all up and let air into it. This helps to keep the soil healthy. You can watch worms at work by making a wormery.

1. Take a large glass jar and fill it with three layers of different soils – gravel or sand, mud from a stream and ordinary soil will do.

2. Add a layer of leaves. Then put four or five worms on top.

3. Wrap black paper round your wormery to keep it dark and make sure the soil is kept moist. Check it after a day or two to see what has happened.

41

City Living

Modern cities are really jungles of concrete and tarmac. Yet a city habitat is very different from a natural habitat such as a wood. Despite this, wildlife can be found even in the centre of the world's busiest cities. Animals are attracted to cities because there is a vast and never-ending supply of free food, such as the food that gets thrown out with our rubbish. Many birds and mammals make their homes in parks and tree-lined roads, whereas animals such as rats and mice live beneath the cities in the sewers and drains.

👁 Eye-Spy

You have to look quite carefully to spot some city dwellers. Old walls may be home to a host of tiny plants and animals. How many creatures can you find living on a wall?

Cities can be home to some unlikely guests including elk, monkeys, raccoons and foxes. Others animals, such as rats and mice, are more common inhabitants.

elk in Scandinavian and Canadian towns

pigeons

fox

rats

mice

vervet monkeys in towns in Africa

storks often nest on rooftops in northern European towns

Polar bears are among the largest visitors to towns – and the most dangerous! Many are attracted by the free supply of food that can be found on rubbish tips.

Do it yourself

Attract birds to your town garden or school grounds by putting out bird food.

To make a coconut cake, melt 250g of lard or suet. Mix in 500g of mixed raisins, sultanas, peanuts, bread and cake crumbs, sunflower seeds and oatmeal. Put the mix into half a coconut shell and let it set before you hang it up outside.

Make a string of monkey nuts by threading the nuts together using a large needle and strong thread.

string of monkey nuts

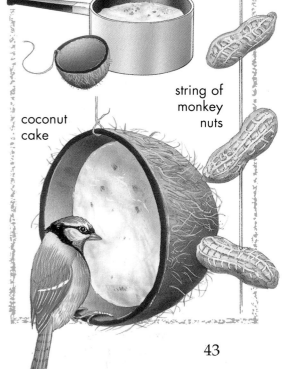

coconut cake

raccoons are found in cities in the USA

43

Life on the Highways

Roads reach almost everywhere. The grassy banks, or verges, are often planted with grass and trees to make them look attractive. Although there is pollution from car fumes, the verges are usually free from harmful pesticides. So roadsides have formed new habitats for many plants and animals. The plants attract insects, birds and mammals. Some birds feed on dead insects that bounce off car windscreens. Other birds and foxes feed on animals that are killed on the road.

kestrel

fox

Beware!
Special road signs are used to warn drivers about animals crossing the road. This safeguards the animals but also prevents drivers from having accidents.

Roadside verges attract many plants and animals that do not mind living so close to traffic.

bee

Save a Toad

Every Spring, toads travel to their breeding ponds. They often have to cross roads, and many get killed. Now, people help toads by carrying them safely across the roads.

rabbit

butterfly

hedgehog

vole

Do it yourself

Make a highway habitat mobile.

1. Trace the shapes off this page and transfer them on to stiff card. You will need one hawk, four mice and two of each of the fruits. Cut your shapes out.

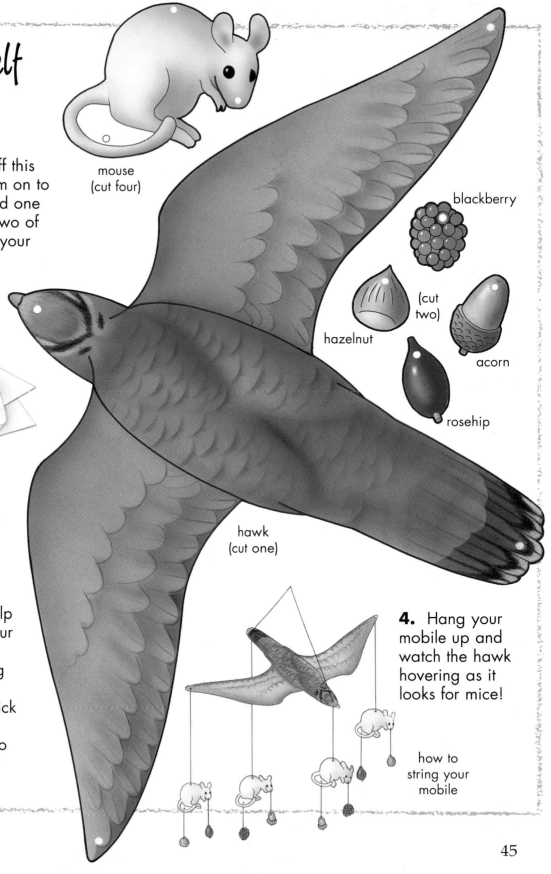

mouse
(cut four)

blackberry

hazelnut

(cut two)

acorn

rosehip

hawk
(cut one)

2. Paint or colour the shapes on both sides. Use a felt tip pen to add the details.

3. Ask an adult to help you pierce holes in your shapes as marked on the pattern. Then string your mobile together using a needle and thick thread. Follow the diagram on the right to see where each of the pieces should go.

4. Hang your mobile up and watch the hawk hovering as it looks for mice!

how to string your mobile

45

Endangered Wildlife

Many plants and animals have disappeared completely from Earth. That is, they have become extinct. Sometimes this happens naturally. Dinosaurs may have died out because of a sudden change in climate. But many species are now extinct because of humans. Destruction of habitat is the biggest threat to wildlife. It has made animals such as the giant panda become endangered. This means that there are only a few thousand individuals, or even fewer, left in the world.

Special organizations such as Greenpeace try to protect endangered animals. Here, they are trying to stop whaling.

Extinct!

The dodo was a large flightless bird that lived on Mauritius. An easy catch for sailors, the last one was killed in 1700.

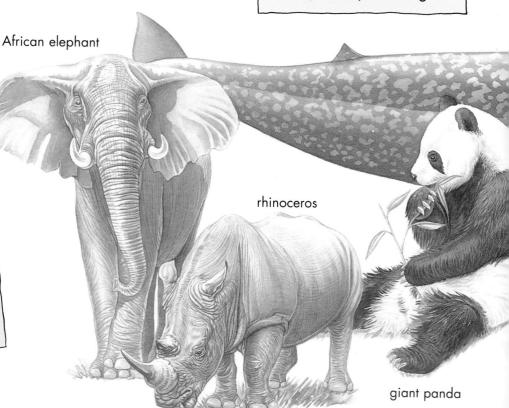

African elephant

rhinoceros

giant panda

Running Wild

Wolves were once a common sight in Europe and the USA. But they caught sheep and cattle, so they were shot by farmers. They are now being reintroduced to some of the places where they once roamed wild.

Countryside Code

Many of us can do little to help tigers and whales, but we can all help to conserve wildlife closer to home by following a few simple rules when we go into the countryside.

Many well-known animals are endangered. If these animals are not protected, and their habitats conserved, they may soon disappear forever. Imagine what the world would be like without tigers, elephants, pandas and whales!

blue whale

orang-utan

Siberian tiger

- Do not pick any wild flowers, even if there are plenty of them.
- Keep to the footpaths so you do not trample wild flowers.
- Keep your dog on a lead if there are animals or nesting birds about.
- Close gates so that farm animals do not escape.

Zoos Today

For a long time, zoos were simply places where animals were kept in small cages to entertain the public. The modern zoo, however, has a far more important role. Many zoos keep endangered animals. This is often the only way to stop an animal becoming extinct. The zoos breed them in special enclosures. Eventually, they may be able to release some of the animals back into the wild.

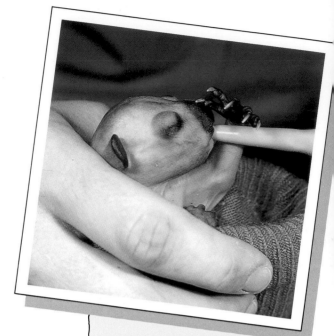

Sometimes a mother animal abandons her baby, so zoo-keepers have to rear it by hand. This baby koala is only a few days old.

Modern zoos have large enclosures where the animals can live together. The brown bear above is catching salmon from a stream in its enclosure. Older zoos have small brick cages. Animals have little room to move around and are often kept on their own for all of their lives.

POLLUTION AND WASTE

What is Pollution?

Every day we pour harmful substances into our environment, such as poisonous gases, chemicals and rubbish. Harmful substances that damage the environment are called pollution. Most pollution comes from factories and tranport but, as you will see, we all contribute to it in some way. It is difficult to stop pollution, but it must be done before we cause too much damage.

When rocks are dug up from quarries to make new roads and buildings, ugly holes are left that spoil the beauty of the countryside. Scars in the landscape are a form of visual pollution.

Do it yourself

Make some simple pollution testers.

To test rain for pollution, line a funnel with a coffee filter. Put the funnel in a jar and place your tester outside in the rain. Check the filter paper after an hour to see how dirty it is. Take a closer look through a magnifying glass.

On a dry day, smear petroleum jelly inside three metal lids. Place one lid inside your home, one in the street and one in the park. After a day, compare them to see how much dirt has collected. Which place is dirtiest?

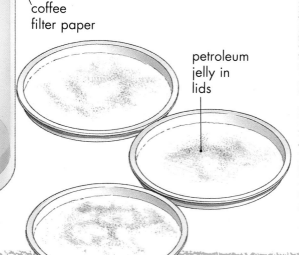

rainwater

coffee filter paper

petroleum jelly in lids

magnifying glass

air transport

spraying fertilizer

Poisonous gases from factories and transport pollute the air. Rubbish, sewage and chemicals poured into rivers and oceans pollute our water. Mining for rock, metals and coal causes water and visual pollution. Spraying fields with pesticides and fertilizers pollutes the land.

factory fumes

road transport

coal mine

👁 Eye-Spy

Do a pollution survey by seeing how much litter, noise and smelly fumes there are in your street. Write down your results on a chart. Then try the park, the high street and your garden. Which place is the most polluted?

Pollution even happens in your home and your street. Rubbish spills from waste bins and cars pump out exhaust fumes.

car exhaust fumes

rubbish

Dirty Air

Every minute of every day we breathe in air. Clean air is essential for life. It is a mixture of gases, mainly oxygen and nitrogen with small amounts of carbon dioxide, plus water. Air has no colour or smell, except when it is polluted. Dirty air can affect the health of humans, animals and plants, and can even damage buildings. Industry and transport produce almost all the pollution in our air, releasing millions of tonnes of harmful gases and soot into the environment each year.

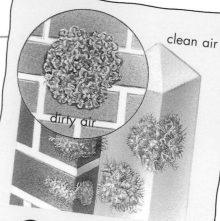

clean air

dirty air

👁 Eye-Spy

Lichens are crispy plant-like growths found on trees, rocks and buildings. You can test for air pollution by finding out which type grow near your home. Thick, hairy lichens only grow in clean air. Flat lichens (inset) can grow in dirty air.

The Air Cycle

All the oxygen in our air comes from trees and other plants. They take carbon dioxide from the air and use it to make food, giving off oxygen as they do so. Animals breathe in the oxygen and release carbon dioxide which the plants use to make more food. But factories and homes burn fuels for heat which uses up oxygen and releases too much carbon dioxide and other, poisonous gases into the air.

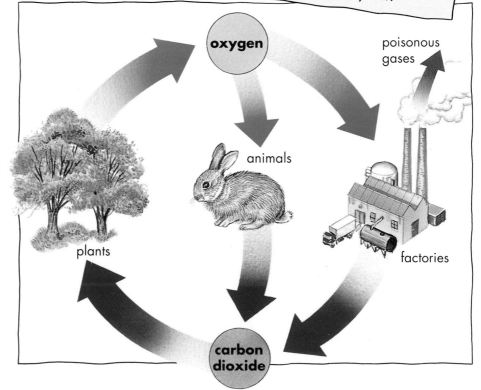

oxygen

poisonous gases

animals

plants

factories

carbon dioxide

Do it yourself

Burning coal to make electricity, petrol to power cars, or gas for heating, all pollutes the air. Ask an adult to help you see how much dirt is made even when a candle burns.

Simply light a candle and bring a heat-proof dish down over the yellow part of the flame for 30 seconds. Move the dish from side to side as you do so. Now look at the underside of your dish.

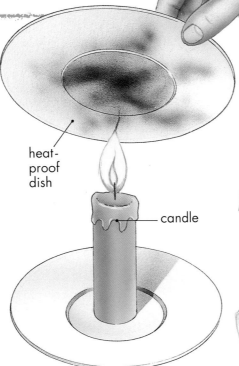

heat-proof dish

candle

How It Works

The black sooty carbon that collects on the underside of the dish is produced when the wax of the candle burns. This carbon usually goes up into the air so you do not see it. Gases are also produced but you don't see them either.

Polluting Our Body

Ask someone who smokes to take a puff from a cigarette without inhaling, then to breathe the smoke out through a white tissue. The black mark on the tissue is a substance called 'tar' which is produced as the tobacco burns. This normally collects in a layer inside the smoker's lungs.

Factory chimneys pump out dirty fumes which are carried far away by the wind.

Rain That Burns

Sometimes rain contains chemicals called acids that can harm wildlife and damage buildings. Acids cause so much harm because they can 'burn' into materials. Acid rain forms when sulphur dioxide and nitrogen dioxide, produced by burning fuel, are released into the air. The two gases mix with water to form a weak acid which falls as rain. Winds may carry the rain far away from the source of pollution. Millions of trees in Europe and North America are now dying from acid rain damage.

Salmon at Risk

Salmon are the first fish to be affected by acid rain. The acid causes aluminium to be washed from the soil into rivers and lakes where it affects the fish's gills.

The gases that cause acid rain are released by power stations, factories and transport. When the acid rain falls to the ground it is taken up by tree roots which eventually causes the trees to die. The acid rain may also drain into lakes and rivers.

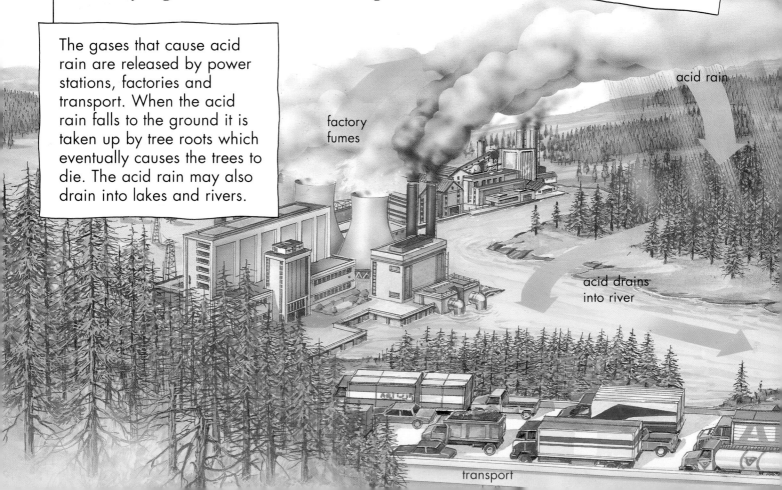

acid rain

factory fumes

acid drains into river

transport

Do it yourself

See how acids can damage plants.

Dip some leaves in a small jar of vinegar and then leave them with their stalks in the vinegar for a few days.

How It Works

Vinegar is a weak kind of acid. The acid damages the leaf from both the inside and the outside, so the leaf soon goes brown and dies.

leaves damaged by acid

vinegar

healthy tree

damaged tree

👁 Eye-Spy

Look around at the trees where you live – in your garden, park or road. Can you see any signs of damage by acid rain? This picture shows you what to look for.

This stone figure (above) has been damaged by acid rain, making it difficult to see the features of the head and body.

More Things To Try

This experiment shows how quickly an acid can eat into rocks. Chalk is used because it is similar to the kinds of rock used on buildings, such as sandstone and limestone, only it is softer. Just put a piece of chalk into a dish of vinegar and watch what happens. Vinegar is stronger than acid rain, so it eats away the chalk much faster than acid rain would.

vinegar

chalk

Cleaning Up Our Act

Probably the biggest causes of air pollution are oil, gas and coal. If we burned fewer of these fuels (called fossil fuels) then we would reduce pollution. There are many laws which control the amount of pollution a factory or car can produce. But it would be better still if we used alternative, cleaner sources of energy, such as solar, wind or water power. As well as causing less pollution, these kinds of energy are renewable – that is, they will not run out. Fossil fuels, on the other hand, are non-renewable and will run out one day.

Switch Off Engines

Cars stuck in traffic jams pump out a lot of air pollution. This sign asks drivers to turn off their car engines while they wait at traffic lights, in order to cut down air pollution.

Alternative Energy

We can make electricity using any one of these alternative sources of energy. Hydroelectric dams built across fast-flowing rivers use the power of water to make electricity. Hot rocks deep in the ground can be used to heat water. This is called geothermal power. Many places in the world have strong winds that can be used to turn the blades of wind generators. And energy from the Sun can be trapped using solar panels.

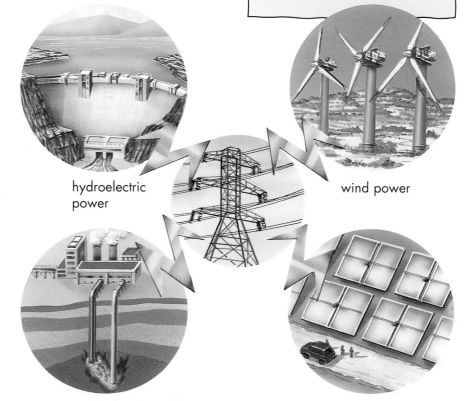

hydroelectric power

wind power

geothermal power

solar power

How Can We Help?

We can help to reduce air pollution by using less electricity and petrol.

- Walk or use public transport instead of a car.
- Give friends a lift on regular journeys such as going to school.
- Turn off lights, the TV and other electrical items when they are not in use.
- Use low-energy light bulbs at home.

Powering Cars

In the future, electric cars will be a common sight on our roads. However, the batteries of an electric car have to be 'recharged' regularly to replace the energy that has been used up. The car batteries could be recharged using solar energy which would mean little pollution and less cost.

electric car

battery recharger

solar panels

Do it yourself

The Sun's heat energy is absorbed, or taken up, by some colours and reflected by others. Find out which colour absorbs most heat and would be best for heating water in a solar panel.

1. Cut some pieces of card about 10cm square. Make each one a different colour – black, white, plus yellow, red, or green. Lay the cards out in the Sun and feel them as they warm up. Which one warms up the quickest?

2. Put an ice cube on each piece of card. Which one melts the quickest and which one melts the slowest?

How It Works

Black is best at absorbing heat from the Sun, so the black card warms up fastest. White reflects the Sun's heat so the white card takes longest. The other colours only absorb some of the heat. A black material is used in solar panels to trap the Sun's heat.

New Forms of Power

Scientists are always trying to find new sources of energy that will not cause pollution. One experiment being carried out in Loch Ness, in Scotland, uses floating bags called clams to trap the power of the waves and make electricity for local homes. The clams shown here are only one-fourteenth of their full size. Maybe in the future we will be using clams to supply homes across the world with electricity.

Do it yourself

Use the power of the wind to spin this fun pinwheel.

1. Cut a piece of paper about 15cm square. Snip in towards the centre from each corner as shown. Fold four opposite corners over to the centre and glue them down, overlapping them slightly.

2. Thread a pin through the centre of your wheel and push it into an eraser on top of a pencil. Now see how the wind can make it spin.

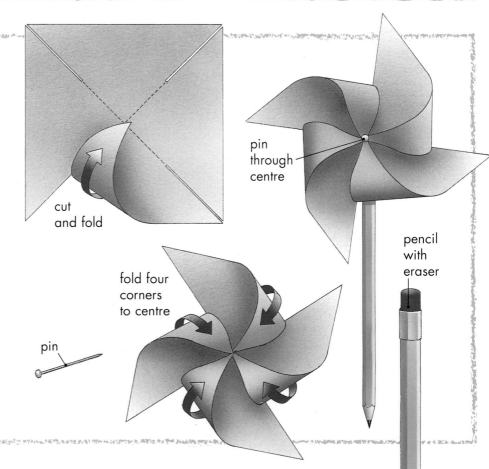

cut and fold

fold four corners to centre

pin

pin through centre

pencil with eraser

Holes in the Sky

The atmosphere is an envelope of air, 500km thick, that completely surrounds the Earth. About 25km up is a thin layer known as the ozone layer. Ozone is a special form of oxygen. It is very important because it protects the Earth against harmful 'ultraviolet' rays from the Sun. But the ozone is being destroyed by chemicals called CFCs (chlorofluorocarbons) that have escaped into the atmosphere. The damage is worst over Antarctica, where the CFCs are eating a hole in the ozone layer.

Banned!

CFCs were once used in refrigerators, aerosol cans and some types of packaging such as burger boxes. Fortunately, they have now been banned from use.

CFCs moving upwards from the Earth make the ozone layer over Antarctica very thin. This is called the ozone hole. Harmful ultraviolet light, most of which is usually blocked by the ozone layer, can get through the hole to reach the Earth's surface.

Sun

ultraviolet rays

CFCs move upwards

Too much ultraviolet light is harmful because it can cause skin cancer. Sunbathers use sun cream to protect their skin.

59

Things Are Hotting Up

The Earth's atmosphere acts rather like a blanket, trapping in heat and keeping the Earth warm. Without this blanket, the Earth would be frozen and lifeless. The heat is trapped by gases that act like the glass of a greenhouse, letting in the heat but preventing it from getting out again. The gases are known as greenhouse gases. Unfortunately, the amount of these gases in the atmosphere is increasing as a result of pollution. The gases are trapping more heat and the Earth is getting hotter.

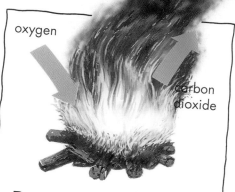

oxygen

carbon dioxide

Burning Fuels

When we burn fuels such as coal, oil and wood, oxygen is used up and carbon dioxide is released. Carbon dioxide is one of the greenhouse gases.

Greenhouse Effect

When heat from the Sun hits the Earth, some of the heat is absorbed. This keeps the Earth and its atmosphere warm. Only a small amount of heat escapes back into Space – most of it is trapped by the greenhouse gases. As the amount of greenhouse gases increases, so the Earth is getting warmer. This may affect the world's climate. Parts of the polar ice caps could melt, the level of the sea could rise and low-lying countries might be flooded.

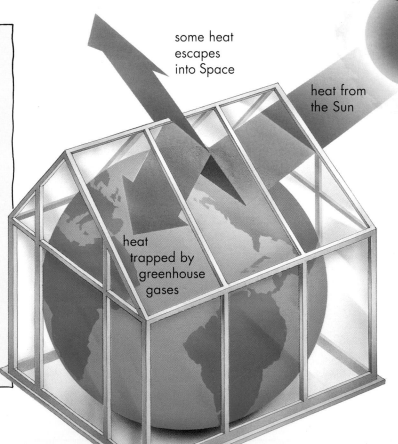

some heat escapes into Space

heat from the Sun

heat trapped by greenhouse gases

Greenhouse Gases

Carbon dioxide is one of the most important greenhouse gases. But methane also adds to the effect. Cows produce methane, and as more people keep more cows so the level of methane is going up. CFCs are also greenhouse gases, so they too are helping to heat up the atmosphere.

Do it yourself

Do this test to see how the greenhouse effect works.

1. Lay a thermometer outside on a sunny day and read the temperature after five minutes.

2. Now put the thermometer inside a clear plastic bag. Puff out the bag with your hands to let lots of air inside, then close the opening and seal it with tape.

3. Leave the bag in the sun for five minutes and then read the temperature of the air inside the bag. Is it higher than your previous reading?

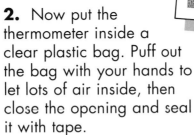

heat from the Sun

plastic bag

thermometer

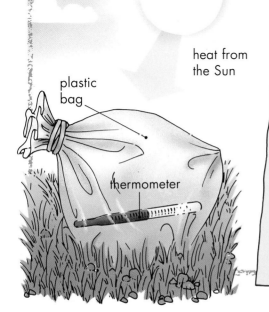

How It Works

The air inside the bag gets warmer than the air outside because the layer of plastic traps the Sun's heat inside. This is similar to the way greenhouse gases trap heat from the Sun inside the Earth's atmosphere, making it warmer.

Is Greenland Green?

Today, Greenland is covered in thick ice. But when it was named by the Vikings long ago it was much warmer and the land was green. Maybe it is normal to have warm periods, and we are worrying unnecessarily about the greenhouse effect.

Polluting Our Water

All animals and plants need a supply of clean water to survive. You may think we have plenty of water, but only a fraction of it is fresh water that we can use, and we are polluting this in the same way as we are damaging the atmosphere. When pollutants such as oil and chemical wastes are poured into water they are soon carried away by the tides or by the flow of the river, and are extremely difficult to remove. One of the most damaging forms of oil pollution in water comes from waste car oil that has been poured down the drain.

👁 Eye-Spy

Next time you go near a river or stream, look out for signs of pollution, such as detergents frothing up with foam, oil floating on the water, old tyres, bottles and tin cans, or dead fish.

As a river winds its way to the sea many different chemicals may enter its waters. Harmful chemicals may seep out of landfill sites (where rubbish is buried). Pesticides and fertilizers may drain into it from farmlands. And sewage from local towns may be poured in. In most countries, sewage now has to be treated before it is emptied into rivers.

landfill site

Rock-Pooling

Looking for animals and plants in rock pools on the beach is great fun. If you find lots of wildlife, you know you are looking at an unpolluted beach.

Banned!

In the past, many countries dumped poisonous wastes and sewage at sea. There are now international laws to stop this happening, and people have to find less harmful ways of getting rid of waste. Even so, some illegal dumping still goes on.

Factories produce a lot of dirty water, much of which ends up in nearby rivers.

Oil spills from ships and oil tankers at sea can cause terrible harm to wildlife.

factories

sewage

farming

oil spillage

Do it yourself

Do these simple tests to see how oil spills can be removed from water.

1. Fill a bowl with water and pour several drops of cooking oil into it. Watch how the oil floats to the surface in a blob.

2. Push the oil about with a spoon handle. Try breaking it up and then joining it back together again.

3. Now dip a small piece of white paper into the water where the oil is lying. See how the oil disappears off the surface of the water and the paper gradually changes colour.

4. Pour a few more drops of cooking oil into the water. Then add a couple of drops of washing-up liquid (which is a detergent) and see what happens.

👁 Eye-Spy

Next time it rains, look at the side of the road for puddles with swirling colours of pink, purple, blue and yellow. These mini oil slicks are made by car oil spreading out over the water's surface.

How It Works

Oil always floats on water. The paper absorbs the oil from the surface of the water, changing colour as it does so. In the same way, when a tanker spills oil on the sea, layers of absorbent material are floated on the surface of the water to soak up the oil.

Detergents such as washing-up liquid break up the blob of oil and spread it out in a thin layer over the surface of the water. Detergents can be used to clean up oil spills at sea. Unfortunately, they can also harm wildlife.

Down on the Farm

Farming has changed over the last 200 years. In the past, the fields were small and horses were used to pull machinery. Today, huge fields stretch as far as the eye can see, and powerful combine harvesters and tractors have taken over. Often the same crop is grown on the land for many years, and chemicals are used to increase the yield (output). This type of 'intensive' farming can cause pollution and harm wildlife.

Chemical Sprays

Farmers spray fertilizers on their crops to help them grow fast and pesticides to kill off wildlife that might damage them. But these chemicals cause pollution.

Many farm animals never see a field. They are kept crowded together in special barns. Their waste, called slurry, can pollute rivers, so it must be disposed of carefully.

In the 1930s, farms in Midwest USA were hit by a long drought. With huge fields and so few trees, there was nothing to stop strong winds blowing away the dry soil. This created a vast dust bowl that could not be farmed.

Intercropping

Sometimes organic farmers control pests and improve the yield by growing two different crops together in the same field, for example maize with beans. This method of farming is called intercropping.

Organic Farming

Although it does not produce as much food as intensive farming, organic farming is much better for the land. The fields are smaller and more trees are allowed to grow. Farmers do not use chemical sprays that cause pollution. And farm animals are free to roam.

Each year, organic farmers 'rotate' their crops. That is, they change the crop grown in each field. This stops the build-up of pests and disease. They keep their soil healthy by mixing in lots of animal manure. As well as feeding the crops, the manure holds the soil together so it does not blow away. The animals are free-range, so they can wander in the fields instead of being kept in barns.

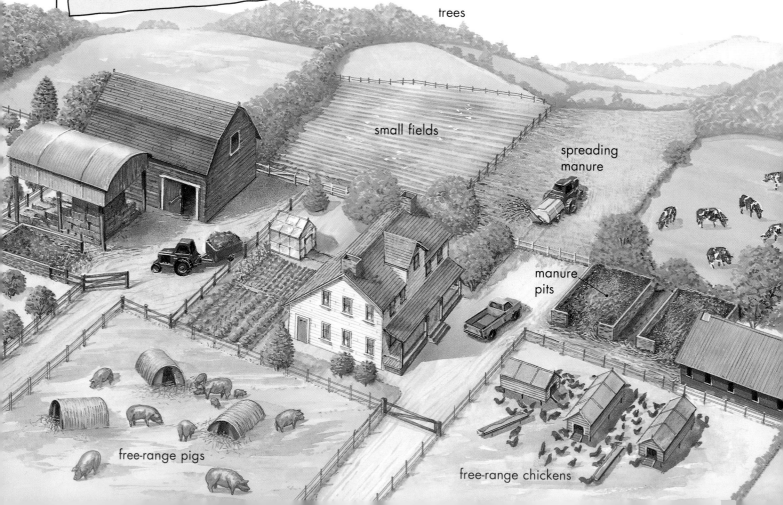

trees

small fields

spreading manure

manure pits

free-range pigs

free-range chickens

👁 Eye-Spy

Milk, eggs, meat, fruits and vegetables can all be produced by organic farming methods. See how many different types of organic foods you can see in your local shops.

Making a Choice

Fruits and vegetables in shops often look perfect. This is because they have been sprayed with chemicals to kill any pests that might spoil their appearance.

Organically-grown fruits and vegetables are not sprayed. They do not look as perfect but they taste just as good, if not better! Which type would you buy if you had a choice?

Organic farmers use natural fertilizers such as manure and compost to feed their crops. These are just as rich as chemical fertilizers but they are not as polluting.

produce grown using chemical sprays

organically-grown produce

Getting Rid of Waste

We produce more waste today than ever before, so it is important that we get rid of it safely, without harming the environment. People throw away ten times their own body weight in rubbish every year. This is either buried in the ground or burned. Every day litres of dirty water disappear down the plug hole. The water has to be treated before it can be pumped back into rivers and oceans. Industry also produces waste. This is usually dumped in a landfill, poured into rivers and seas, or burned.

Mountains of Litter

Litter is a form of waste. It gets everywhere, even on Mount Everest where climbers drop their rubbish on the mountainside.

Where It Comes From

Waste matter comes from many different sources. Factories produce liquid and solid wastes, as well as gases. Intensive animal farming produces slurry. And every home produces dirty water and sewage, along with household rubbish.

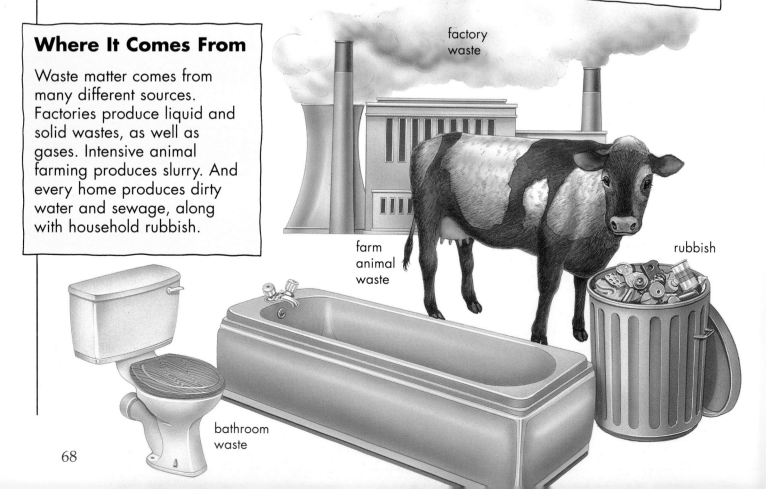

factory waste

farm animal waste

rubbish

bathroom waste

Toxic (poisonous) industrial waste is difficult to get rid of safely. Some of it has to undergo special treatment before it can be put back into the environment. This can be very expensive.

Water pouring out of a waste pipe into a river is a common sight in many countries. This water often contains chemicals that can harm animals and plants.

Scoop the Poop!

Dog mess is a form of waste that can be very unpleasant. People can help to keep our parks and streets clean by making use of specially provided dog waste bins.

Do it yourself

Organize a 'litter blitz'

Litter is one of the most unnecessary forms of waste. It spoils our environment and harms wildlife. Get together with some friends and clean up your local street, park, school ground or beach. Pick up all the litter you can find, put it in plastic bin liners and throw it away properly. Be sure to wear gloves when handling litter.

How Can We Help?

Try to reduce litter and waste where you live.

- Don't drop litter.
- Make and display a poster in your window asking people to keep your neighbourhood a 'litter-free zone'.
- Organize your friends and neighbours to do a litter blitz.
- Don't allow your dog to foul the pavements or local park. If it does, be sure to clear it up.

Pollution at Home

Many of the substances we use at home can cause pollution. Cleaners can be particularly harmful. One of the most polluting is bleach which is used to kill germs. And detergents often contain chemicals called phosphates that can pollute local rivers and lakes. Artificial perfumes in furniture polishes and air fresheners pollute the air. Even medicines can be harmful if they get into the environment. To help reduce pollution, many household substances are now made to be 'environmentally friendly'.

Keeping Clean

Clean bodies are healthy, and to stay clean we use an array of shampoos, soaps and deodorants. But the colours and perfumes often added to these products to make them feel good are not really necessary and can sometimes irritate the skin.

Here are just some of the harmful substances you may have at home. Read the labels on the cleaners to see if the ones you have are environmentally friendly.

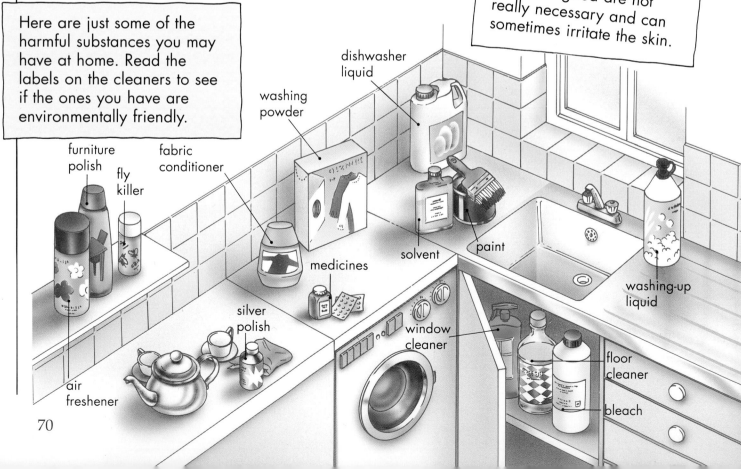

furniture polish

fly killer

fabric conditioner

washing powder

dishwasher liquid

solvent

paint

washing-up liquid

medicines

silver polish

window cleaner

floor cleaner

bleach

air freshener

70

RUBBISH AND RECYCLING

What a Waste!

People produce loads of rubbish. Throughout the world, we create a billion tonnes of it each year. Even cavemen produced it. Their caves soon filled with old bones, wood and other waste, so eventually they had to move to a new cave. Today we throw away more rubbish than ever before. But many of the things we think of as rubbish are not waste at all. They are made from valuable materials taken from the environment (called raw materials) that *could* be used again.

Wasted Cars

In the USA, over seven milllion cars are scrapped each year. The metals can be recycled, but that still leaves a lot of waste, including millions of tyres.

restaurant waste

litter

garage waste

household waste

Instead of being thrown away, much of the rubbish seen here could be reused, or recycled, to make new things. This would mean taking fewer raw materials from our environment.

Do it yourself

Do a packaging survey.

Much of the rubbish we throw out comes from packaging – the materials used to wrap food and other goods we buy from shops. Next time you or a member of your family go shopping, count the number of layers of wrapping on some of the items. Packaging holds the goods together and makes them look attractive. But often you will find there are lots of unnecessary layers.

chocolate wrappers

lid

tray

protective layer

paper

base

cakes may have up to four layers

lid

cellophane

cake

base

tray

a box of chocolates may have up to six layers of packaging

box

tray

toys usually have few layers

toy

office waste

industrial waste

today

20 years ago

These are just some of the many things we think of as waste. But the real waste is throwing away so many valuable materials such as paper, glass, wood and metals. Even kitchen waste can be reused.

shop waste

Getting Lighter

In the last 20 years, the packaging used for supermarket goods has become one-third lighter. This helps to cut down on waste and saves energy.

73

Where Does It Go?

Each week, our rubbish is put out in dustbins to be collected and taken away. Much of it ends up being buried in a landfill. This is a big hole in the ground, such as a disused quarry or sand pit. But burying rubbish takes up a lot of space and spoils the countryside. Sometimes the rubbish is taken to an incinerator where it is burned. The heat may be used to make electricity for local homes. But burning it produces harmful fumes that pollute the air.

Energy from Waste

Burning rubbish to make electricity is a useful way of getting rid of waste. One dustbinful of rubbish can generate as much electricity as a bag of coal.

Not all rubbish is wasted. Rotting rubbish gives off a gas called methane which can be burned to make electricity. Kitchen and garden waste can be made into compost and sprayed on fields. And many materials can be recycled.

burned in an incinerator

methane gas used to make electricity

buried in landfill

used as compost

recycled to make new goods

Rubbish put in a landfill is squashed down before more rubbish is placed on top. Eventually, the hole is filled completely. Then it may be covered with soil and turned into a park or sports ground.

Recycling is a good way to help our planet. It saves materials, energy, and land that might otherwise be used as landfill. It also reduces pollution.

Do it yourself

Do a charity clear-out.

Charities collect a wide range of items that might otherwise get thrown away. Find out what your local charity shop collects and have a charity clear-out at home. Instead of being burned, your waste could end up helping someone.

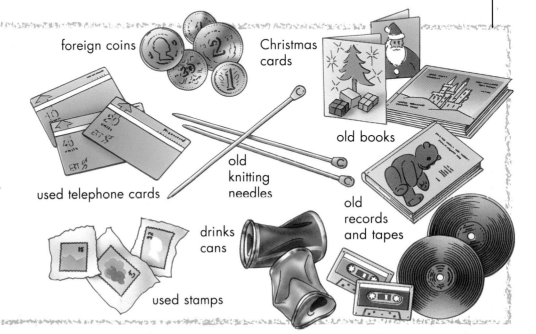

foreign coins

Christmas cards

used telephone cards

old knitting needles

old books

old records and tapes

drinks cans

used stamps

Nature's Recycling

Have you noticed that you never see huge piles of dead trees and animals in woodlands? This is because natural materials quickly decompose (break down) and are recycled. These materials are said to be biodegradable. Nature is very good at recycling, so nothing goes to waste. Minibeasts, earthworms, fungi and microscopic bacteria are important because their job is to break down the wastes. They are called decomposers.

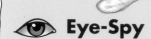 **Eye-Spy**

Look out for waste that is biodegradable. Apple cores, dead leaves, old clothes, cardboard boxes and newspapers will all eventually rot or get eaten.

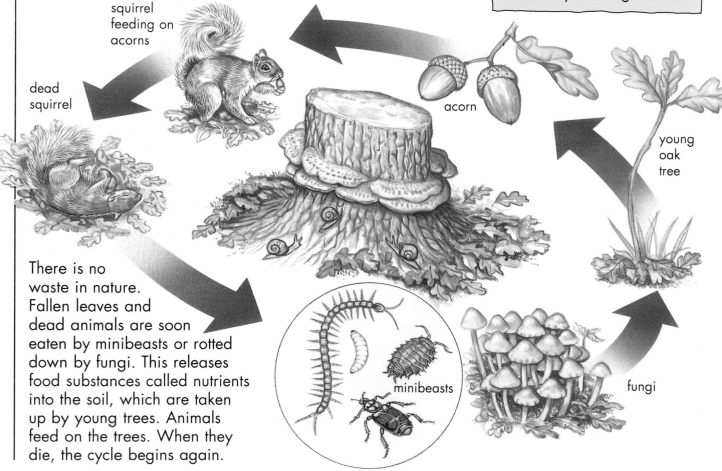

squirrel feeding on acorns

dead squirrel

acorn

young oak tree

There is no waste in nature. Fallen leaves and dead animals are soon eaten by minibeasts or rotted down by fungi. This releases food substances called nutrients into the soil, which are taken up by young trees. Animals feed on the trees. When they die, the cycle begins again.

minibeasts

fungi

Do it yourself

Catch some minibeast decomposers using this simple method.

1. Cut a piece of thick paper about 30cm x 20cm. Roll it up to make a funnel shape and tape it together. The hole at the bottom should be about 1cm across.

folding paper into cone

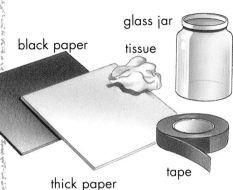

glass jar

black paper

tissue

thick paper

tape

2. Put some damp tissue in the bottom of a glass jar and wrap the jar with a piece of black paper. Put your funnel in the jar.

3. Collect some leaf litter from under some trees. (Leaf litter is a damp mixture of rotten leaves and soil.)

Worms at Work

Worms are good recyclers. They feed on dead and rotting matter, such as leaves, that they find on the ground. This helps to break the matter down so it can be reused by plants.

4. Fill your funnel with leaf litter and leave the jar sitting under a strong light from a table lamp for two hours. Minibeasts prefer dark damp places, so the ones in your leaf litter will try to crawl away from the heat and light of the lamp. They will soon fall through the bottom of the funnel into the jar.

More Things To Try

Build a home for your decomposers by turning a large jar on its side. Make breathing holes in the lid and put some soil, rotten wood and leaf litter inside, along with your minibeasts. Add plenty of food such as apple or potato peel and keep the soil damp. Then cover the jar with a dark cloth. Return the creatures to their natural habitat after a few days.

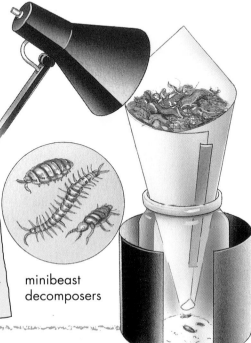

minibeast decomposers

decomposers' home

Rubbish That Won't Rot

If you left a plastic bag, a glass bottle, or an aluminium can outside, it would stay there, unchanged, for hundreds of years. This is because plastic, glass and metal are non-biodegradable – they will never rot. Of course, it is important for some materials to be non-biodegradable. Buildings materials, glass and many plastics must stay intact to do their job properly. But when they are no longer needed, these materials are difficult to get rid off.

nuts   nails

Much of the rubbish we throw out each week will never rot. We have to keep creating new landfill sites to take it all. One day, our planet could become one big rubbish tip!

cling film

plastic bottle

polystyrene box

drinks can

Do it yourself

Do a litter survey to find out how much litter there is in your street, around your school and in your local park.

Draw a chart like the one shown below. Mark on your chart how much litter you find in each place and what kind of litter it is. Clear the litter up as you go by putting it in a bin liner. Be sure to wear gloves when you touch litter.

	STREET	PARK	GARDEN
GLASS	LHT I	IIII	II
PAPER	LHT III	IIII	
PLASTIC	III	II	LHT

How Can We Help?

- Never drop litter – rubbish that is made of plastics, polystyrene, metals and glass will not rot away.
- Do a litter survey like the one here, and organize a 'litter blitz' to clear it all up.

crisp
packet

glass

cooking foil

👁 Eye-Spy

Because most litter does not rot, it will stay in our environment for many years unless it is cleared up. Check the dates on litter, such as crisp packets, to see how old it is.

batteries

Litter gets everywhere, from our streets to our beaches, and it is not a pretty sight. People who drop non-biodegradable waste outdoors are spoiling the environment for everyone else.

Do it yourself

Find out which rubbish is biodegradable and which is not by doing this simple test.

1. Collect some yoghurt pots or plastic cups and fill them with damp soil.

2. Find several bits of man-made rubbish and several bits of natural rubbish. Bury each object in a pot and identify it with a label. Leave the pots somewhere cool and damp for a couple of weeks, then dig up the objects to see if they have rotted or changed at all.

How It Works

The natural rubbish will have started to decompose or may have rotted away altogether because it is biodegradable. The man-made rubbish does not decompose and will not have changed at all. Luckily, we can recycle much of our non-biodegradable rubbish so that it can be used again.

yoghurt
pots

soil

banana skin

paper

leaf

marble

lid

nail

sweet wrapper

potato peel

79

Waste Not, Want Not

It is very wasteful to throw things away if they can be reused or recycled. Raw materials have to be taken from the environment to make new things, which uses energy and causes pollution. So, the more we throw away, the more the environment will be harmed. The number of materials we can recycle is increasing all the time. Once, only glass and metal were recyclable. Nowadays, we can also recycle paper, cardboard, rags, batteries, plastics and much more.

👁 Eye-Spy

Next time you empty a bottle or drinks can, finish a comic or tear a T-shirt, think about whether the leftovers can be recycled.

Christmas Recycling

Instead of throwing out your old Christmas tree with the rubbish, take it to a recycling centre where you may be able to get it chipped into tiny pieces for reuse as garden compost.

30% waste paper and cardboard

30% kitchen waste

10% metal

10% glass

8% plastics

4% old clothes

8% other materials, including dust

This diagram shows the different amounts of waste that get thrown out in our rubbish each week. If we were more careful, we could recycle three-quarters of our household waste.

Do it yourself

Find out how much rubbish your family produces in a week and sort it into bags ready for recycling.

1. Find seven plastic carrier bags and tape a piece of scrap paper on to each one so you can write down what it contains. You will need a bag for each of the following: metal, paper, cardboard, plastics and polystyrene, glass, old clothes and fabrics, and food scraps.

2. Sort your rubbish into the different bags and see how much you collect in a week. How does your rubbish compare with the amounts shown in the diagram opposite?

sorting rubbish into different bags

Nothing Wasted

The people in many poorer countries are far better at recycling than we are. They cannot afford to throw away things like plastic bags and bottles, which we take for granted. All their rubbish is carefully sorted so that any useful materials can be recycled. This couple is collecting cardboard boxes for recycling in Jakarta, in Indonesia.

How Can We Help?

We should all try to cut down on the amount of rubbish we produce. The best way to do so is to remember the three Rs – that is, *reduce, reuse* and *recycle*.

We can reduce waste by buying less in the first place, reuse items such as carrier bags and glass jars instead of throwing them away, and recycle our rubbish so that materials are not wasted.

81

Down the Plug Hole

Every day, we each use litres of water cleaning ourselves and flushing the toilet. We also use water for cooking, and in dishwashers and washing machines, as well as for washing the car. Once we have finished with the water, it disappears down the drain. But that is not the last we see of it. It is then cleaned and recycled so we can use it again. There always seems to be plenty of fresh water. But sometimes, if there has been a drought, there is hardly enough to go round. So we must all try to reduce the amount of water we use.

How Many Times?

In many large cities, water from the tap has been recycled as many as 20 times! But it is still perfectly safe to drink.

Do it yourself

Do a water survey to see how much water is used at home by your family in a day.

Draw a chart like the one here, listing all the things that use up water in your home, such as boiling a kettle, flushing the toilet or having a bath. Mark it on your chart each time someone uses water. How is water used most often? Could you think of ways to use less water?

	How often
Kettle	ℍℍ I
Cooking	II
Washing up	I
Washing Machine	II
Dish Washer	I
Toilet	ℍℍ II
Bath	II
Watering plants	I
Hose pipe	

your home

rain falls

reservoir
supplies
homes
with water

The Water Cycle

treatment
plant

water
evaporates

clean water
pumped into river

Dirty water from your home goes to a treatment plant to be cleaned. Then it is poured into rivers and carried to the sea. Some water evaporates (turns into a gas) and forms clouds. When rainwater falls, it fills up the reservoirs that supply us with water.

Do it yourself

See how quickly water evaporates.

Measure out 50ml of water into each of three different containers – a saucer, a glass and a bottle. Leave them on a sunny windowsill for a day.

From which container has most water disappeared?

How It Works

The water evaporates fastest from the saucer because it has a large surface area open to the air. It takes longest to evaporate from the bottle because there is little surface area open to the air and only a small hole to escape through.

Banks for Bottles

Glass has been used for thousands of years. It is made by heating sand, soda and limestone together at very high temperatures so that they melt and form a liquid. As the liquid cools, it turns into glass. Glass is easy to recycle. The old glass is cleaned and broken up, then it is melted and moulded into shape just like new glass. Recycling means taking fewer raw materials from the ground. It also helps to save energy.

Buying milk and orange juice in returnable glass bottles saves energy and raw materials because the bottles can be reused up to 11 times. A carton can only be used once.

crushing glass

hot glass

glass for recycling

melting glass in furnace

bottle mould

bottle bank

supermarket

filling and capping bottles

Glass from a bottle bank is cleaned and broken up into small pieces called cullet. The cullet is melted down in a furnace and the liquid glass is then poured into a mould and left to cool. The bottles are filled and capped, ready for our supermarket shelves.

A mountain of glass lies waiting to be recycled. Glass is sorted into different colours before it is processed. Clear glass is the most useful because it can be made into all kinds of bottles and jars, but green glass has fewer uses – it is mostly made into wine bottles.

Do it yourself

Instead of recycling it, reuse a glass bottle to make this pretty table decoration.

1. Buy a block of florists' foam from a flower shop and cut off a small piece about 8cm square and 4cm deep.

2. Cut a hole in the middle big enough to fit over the neck of the bottle. Soak the foam in water, then put it over the neck. Now place a candle in the bottle and fill the foam with pretty flowers and ivy. (Do not light the candle without an adult present.)

glass bottle

florist's foam

flowers

candle

85

How Can We Help?

- Take unwanted glass to a bottle bank to be recycled.
- Buy milk, orange juice and yoghurt in reusable glass bottles rather than cartons and pots whenever possible.
- Reuse bottles and jars as containers or vases (see below for ideas).

bathroom tiles

reflective road signs

Not all recycled glass is used to make new bottles and jars. Some is used to make bathroom tiles, bricks, reflective road signs, and fibreglass boats and canoes.

bricks

fibreglass boat

Do it yourself

Make a bottle orchestra.

Collect some empty bottles and jars of all shapes and sizes and wash them out. Fill them with different amounts of water to give a range of notes, then 'play' them by tapping them with a metal spoon. See if you can play any tunes you know.

playing bottle with metal spoon

More Things To Try

Reuse glass bottles and jars by turning them into containers for pens and pencils, flowers, marbles and much more. Paint them with jazzy designs or glue paper scraps or stamps all over them.

Cans Count

Metal food cans have been used for about 200 years. Cans are ideal for storing food and drink for long periods. We use millions of them every day. The metal used in cans is valuable, so recycling is very important. There is no limit to the number of times the metal can be recycled. Steel made from old cans uses just one quarter of the energy that would be needed to make steel from raw materials. Recycling also means digging up fewer raw materials, creating less rubbish and filling up fewer landfills.

What to Recycle?

All sorts of metal items can be recycled, including steel and aluminium food and drinks cans, bottle tops and aluminium foil and frozen food trays.

Cans in Space

Every year, more than 16 billion cans are used in the UK alone. If they could be lined up end to end, they would stretch to the Moon and back twice!

Everything made of steel contains some steel that has been recycled. The steel in a can of beans could end up in a bridge, a car, a knife, or just a simple paper clip.

cutlery

scissors

kitchen knives

refrigerators

paper clips

bridges

cars

Aluminium and Steel Cans

The first cans were made from iron coated with a thin layer of tin, which is why we still call them tin cans. Nowadays cans are made from steel or aluminium. Drinks cans have to be light, so they are made from a very thin sheet of metal. Food cans have to be thicker and stronger so they can protect their contents.

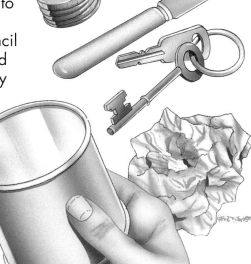

Inside a recycling plant special machines are used to squash aluminium cans into bales. The cans are then melted down and rolled out to form sheet aluminium, ready to be used again.

Eye-Spy

Most drinks cans now have a symbol, or logo, on their side, reminding you to recycle them. Here are some of the logos to look out for.

Do it yourself

Do this simple test to see if a can is made of steel or aluminium.

Steel is magnetic – that is, it is attracted to magnets – and aluminium is not. So hold the can up to a magnet and see if it sticks. If it does, it is made of steel. If it does not, it is made of aluminium.

Check other metal objects to see if they are magnetic, such as needles, keys, pencil sharpeners, knives, foil and bottle tops. If they are, they are made of steel or iron.

magnet

can

88

Saving Energy

The amount of energy needed to make one aluminium can from raw materials is the same as that required to make 20 cans from recycled aluminium.

How Can We Help?

- Take your food and drinks cans to your local recycling centre.
- Encourage your school to get a can bank so you can all collect cans for recycling.
- Don't forget that foil, bottle tops, and take-away metal trays can be recycled too!

Do it yourself

Use a couple of empty food cans and a length of string to make your own 'mobile phone'.

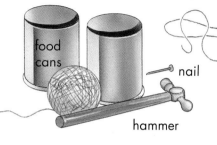

food cans

nail

hammer

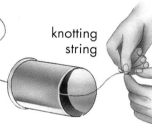

knotting string

string

3. Cut a piece of string 20 metres long. Feed each end through a hole in the base of the cans. Tie the ends off with a knot on the inside.

4. Ask a friend to hold a can up to his or her ear and stand as far away from you as possible. Keeping the string pulled tight, speak into your can and see if your friend can hear you.

1. Ask an adult to file down any sharp edges on the cans. Then wash them out.

2. With an adult's help, make a hole in each can, in the centre of the base, using a hammer and nail.

How It Works

Your voice makes the can vibrate as you speak into it. The vibrations are carried along the string to the other can which also vibrates, reproducing the sound of your voice so your friend can hear you speaking.

89

Recycling Plastics

Plastic is a very useful material that is cheap and easy to make. This is why we use so much of it. In the USA, two and a half million plastic bottles are used every hour! Most plastic is non-biodegradable which makes it difficult to get rid of. The best way is to recycle it and make something new with it. Oil is used to make many plastics, so recycling also saves oil.

LPs are made from plastic. There are millions of unwanted LPs in the world and they are now being collected and turned into cheque cards!

stuffing for furnishings

bin liners

piping

squeezy bottles

plant pots

fencing

Wellington boots

carrier bags

👁 Eye-Spy

These logos are used on plastic packaging to show that it can be recycled. A different number is used for each type of plastic. Can you find these logos on containers in your home?

1 2 3

A surprising range of objects can be made using recycled plastic, from carrier bags and white squeezy bottles to Wellington boots, plant pots and piping.

Do it yourself

Reuse a plastic bottle to make an unusual plant holder. You may need to ask an adult to help you with the cutting.

1. Find an empty 2 litre plastic drinks bottle and peel off the label. Using a felt tip pen, draw two rings around the bottle, one 8cm from the bottom, the other 13cm from the top as shown on the page opposite.

plastic drinks bottle

scissors

small pot plant

Fast Food

Polystyrene fast food containers trap the heat so that the food does not get cold. They once had to be thrown away, but now they can be recycled.

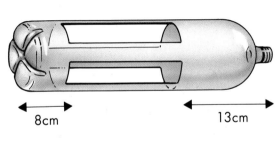

8cm   13cm

2. Draw two lines, 15mm apart, down the length of the bottle between the two rings. Draw three more sets of lines, evenly spacing them round the bottle. Cut out the large rectangles between your lines.

3. Make two holes in the top of the bottle and thread string through to hang up your container. Finally, put a small pot plant inside.

Plastics for recycling are first sorted into the different types. Then they are washed and shredded into tiny pieces, or chips, before being melted down and turned into something new.

How Can We Help?

- Take plastic bottles and other packaging to your local recycling centre.
- Take a plastic carrier bag with you when you go shopping so you don't need to be given a new one.
- Reuse plastic ice cream tubs as sandwich or freezer boxes.
- Use yoghurt pots for mixing paints or glue.

91

Recycle Your Rags

Old clothes and rags should never be thrown away. Just like glass and paper, rags can be recycled. Some fabrics are ripped up to make a substance called 'shoddy'. This is used to make furniture fabrics, blankets, carpets and even new clothes. Other fabrics are turned into stuffing for mattresses, and some are used as wiping cloths for machinery.

New from Old

This girl is wearing an outfit knitted entirely out of recycled wool.

Some old clothes are collected by charities and are resold or sent to poorer countries. A few clothes are burned as rubbish. But the rest can be recycled.

recycled as blankets, furnishing fabrics, carpets and clothes

sent to people in poor countries

burned as rubbish

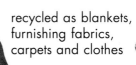

Old woollen clothes are used to make shoddy. First they have to be sorted into colours – sometimes as many as 50 different ones!

recycled as stuffing for mattresses

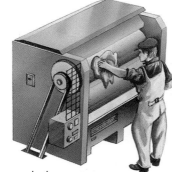

recycled as wiping cloths for factory machinery

92

Index

A

acid rain 32, 54, 55
air cycle 52
air fresheners 70
air pollution 10, 12, 52-53
algal blooms 33, 36
aluminium, recycling 87, 88, 89
anemometers 23
animal habitats 28
animals, endangered 48
artificial perfumes 70
asthma 10
atoms 18

B

bacteria 76
biodegradable materials 76
birds 36, 43
bleach 70
bottle banks 84, 86

C

cancer, skin 59
cans, recycling 87, 88, 89
carbon 53
carbon dioxide 10, 34, 52, 60, 61
carbon monoxide 12
carnivores 30
cars 12-13, 32, 57, 72
catalytic converters 13
CFCs 59
chemical energy 6, 14, 16
chemical fertilizers 67
chemical waste 36, 62
chlorofluorocarbons 59
city habitats 42
coal 15
combustion 16
compost 74
coniferous forests 28
cooling towers 9
coral reefs 28
countryside code 47
crop rotation 66

crops, organic 66, 67
crop-spraying 40, 65

D

deciduous woodlands 28
decomposers 76, 77
dinosaurs 46
dodos 46
dolphins 38
drift nets 38
dust bowls 65
dynamo lights 8

E

electric cars 21
electrical energy 6, 8
electricity 8, 19, 74
endangered animals 48
endangered forests 34-35
energy 6-7, 14, 22, 24, 26, 56
energy saving 17

environmentally friendly products 70

exhaust fumes 12, 13, 51, 56

F

farming 40-41, 65

farming, intensive 65

farming, organic 66

feather damage, testing 39

fertilizers 40, 62, 65

fertilizers, chemical 67

fertilizers, natural 67

fishing lines 36

fission reaction 18

food chains 30, 31

food for energy 7

food webs 31

forests, endangered 34, 35

fossil fuels 14, 17, 56

free-range animals 40, 66, 67

fuels 8, 9, 16, 17, 60

fungi 76

G

garden waste 74

gases, from plants 35

gases, poisonous 51, 52

Geiger counter 19

generators 8

geothermal energy 26

geothermal power 56

geysers 26

glass, recycling 84, 85

glass, returnable 84

grasslands 28

greenhouse gases 10, 60, 61

Greenpeace 46

H

habitat destruction 46

habitats 28, 42

habitats, animal 28

habitats, city 42

heat absorption tests 57

heat energy 18, 20

heat energy, testing 7

herbivores 30

hydroelectric dams 24, 56

I

incinerators 74

intensive farming 65

intercropping 66

K

kestrels 31

kitchen waste 74

L

lakes, polluted 36-37

landfills 62, 68, 75, 78

lichens 52

light energy 20

litter 32, 68, 78, 79

litter blitzes, organising 69

litter surveys 78

Photographs:
Ecoscene (Blowfield, Cooper, Glover, Gryniewicz, Harwood, N. Hawkes, Hibbert, Jones, W. Lowler, J. Millership, E. Needham, E. Schaffer, A. Towse, Wilkinson, Winkley); Evergreen Recycled Fashions; Greenpeace; NHPA (B. Jones, M. Shimlock, E. Soder, R. Tidman, M. Wendler, D. Woodfall); Oxford Scientific Films (L. Lec Rue); Panos Pictures (R. Giling); Robert Harding Picture Library; Science Photo Library (A. Bartel, M. Bond, D. Lovegrove, H. Morgan, U.S. Dept. of Energy); ZEFA (J. Blanco)